IT'S HUMAN
TO GIVE A SH!T

LEARNING CONTENTMENT
IN THE MODERN WORLD

--A TOOLBOOK--
1ST EDITION

BY JOHN MAZZ

This book is intended as a reference volume only, not as a medical manual. The information given here is designed to broaden your perspective and offer different ideas to help you find peace and contentment. It is not intended as a substitute for any treatment that may have been prescribed by your doctor or therapist.

No generative AI was used in writing or editing this book.

THIS BOOK SHALL NOT BE USED FOR ARTIFICIAL INTELLI-GENCE TRAINING WITHOUT EXPRESSED WRITTEN PERMISSION FROM THE AUTHOR. For avoidance of doubt, Author reserves the rights to reproduce and/or otherwise use the Work in any manner for purposes of training artificial intelligence technologies to generate text, including without limitation, technologies that are capable of generating works in the same style or genre as the Work.

For more info on the author's other works and music, follow the QR codes below.

Books

Music

ISBN 979-8-9902146-0-6 (ebook)
ISBN 979-8-9902146-1-3 (paperback)
LCCN: 2024907111
Published by Sapling Ventures, LLC
Cover design by John Mazzanovich, graphic art by Janette Varcholik.
Printed in the United States of America

Thank you for purchasing this book! I truly hope that a few of the ideas here become useful to you. If you would like to recieve a free copy of my Venn diagram of contentment and other free content, please visit my website, www.johnmazzbooks.com and sign up for my email list. And please leave or send a review!

"Enjoying the read! Lots of gold in it and my initial thoughts are that this book is a personal development book for today, now. It acknowledges the current world we are living in which has changed dramatically in the last twenty years. It was time for a new personal development book, for this new era. Your book is full of realistic, useful insights and practical wisdom to not just navigate this changing world, but to thrive in it. "
-- Karletta Marie, Daily Inspired Life

"I love how personal it feels, the writing style feels like you're talking directly to me. You've inspired me! You lit up a fire in my heart to produce, whether it's artwork, writing, etc.
I was on the part where you were emphasizing that writing is good for the soul and I immediately pulled out my journal and wrote after months of not touching it. You motivated me beyond words! I can't wait to purchase a hard cover when it's released."--Adhuresa Bytyqi

"There were a lot of really good nuggets in this book. It was quick and easy to understand...One of the best lines for me was actually straight out of the introduction: "I don't suggest that we stop caring about what other people think, but instead learn to care more about what we, ourselves, think." Mazz also covered what he thought were the 13 keys to contentment which I found on point, as well as the many facets of self-knowledge and acceptance. I also really liked the section at the end with the life tools and reminders. I may list some of them out on my notes app to peek at every morning. Overall, I definitely thought it had a lot of highlights. It was definitely broad on the advice he has in his book, so there's definitely something for everyone in there."--Barbara Hinderer

"The author wrote the book with the intention of passing on advice for his children on how to have a positive, happy life. As a retiree trying to navigate a more divisive, complex world, I found areas in this book to help me reevaluate my outlook on relationships and how I can be more positive and accepting of others. I learned I am never too old to change my perspective!"--Barbara Estevez

This book is for my children, with gratitude to my parents, my sister, my children's mother, many friends, and great thinkers who've inspired me to try to do better. Also great thanks to my friends and supporters who helped me to get this book published.

TABLE OF CONTENTS

TABLE OF CONTENTS

TABLE OF CONTENTS

INTRODUCTION

What Is This Book About?

This book is about being more in control of your own mental and emotional well-being, which includes considerations for personal connections and cultural relations. It's about choosing a perspective that doesn't undermine your ability to have a good day. Of course, not all days will be good days, but being more in control, living in the moment, being grateful, and having a healthier perspective on yourself and the world will help you recover faster and better.

It's also about getting to know yourself–accepting your knowledge and your ignorance. We all carry huge areas of ignorance, not the least of which is not knowing what others think. And the sooner we accept that fact, the better off we all are, individually and collectively. We know what we know. We will learn more, but we will always have ignorance, even if it gets a bit smaller over time. The sooner you accept this fact, the sooner you'll start being curious, learning, being in control of the things you can control, and letting go of the things you can't control. Your problems will seem less overwhelming and much more manageable.

Even though as humans we share a lot of common characteristics, we are all born into a unique combination of hereditary traits and culture of family, community, nation, or religion. We all see the world a little bit differently. This book contains a lot of psychological tools and philosophical perspectives, but you may find some more or less helpful depending on who you are and at what point you are in your life. Focus on the ideas you find useful or interesting.

A lot of talk is made of being happy. I think happiness is a bit unrealistic or even unhealthy to strive for as a constant in your life. I think a better goal is contentment or peace. Life will have its ups and downs, regardless of who and where you are. It's how we are in between those times that defines us the most. Being content is a good place to land between the peaks and valleys.

How Is This Book Different?

There has been a significant movement in the self-help genre towards encouraging people not to care, accept their "inner asshole" and such. These books offer some good advice, but the titles don't send the healthiest message. Humans are hardwired to care, and being an asshole isn't good for anybody. I don't suggest that we stop caring about what other people think, but instead learn to care more about what we, ourselves, think. Sure, part of gaining more control over your mental well-being is learning to accept things you can't control, such as the opinions of others, but we all can cultivate an opinion of ourselves that is well-informed which gives us a more accurate and healthier self-image. This is also critical in making better decisions regarding our actions, reactions, and personal development. The better we know ourselves, the better decisions we can make. This is something we can control and it gives us greater personal agency.

Another difference is that this book, while presenting some classic philosophy and psychology, places it all contextually in how our psychological evolution hasn't yet caught up with our modern era of mass society and technology. This perspective should help people understand how some of their instinctual reactions to various aspects of life are no longer useful but, instead, counterproductive in the modern age. A better understanding of this dynamic can help in gaining control and making changes in how you react to the newer challenges of modern life.

Another different angle in this book regards your worldview. If your view of the world is that of danger, fear, and distrust, then you have been set up for stress, anxiety, and unfulfilling or potentially dysfunctional relationships. This is not to say that you have to see everything as peaches and cream through rose-colored glasses, but if everything you see is doom and gloom, you can't expect to have many good days. Something in between and more realistic is desirable.

Additionally, when you change your worldview, even in slight ways, you are making it your own. You are taking ownership of your perspective. You are freeing yourself to become who you want to be. Something more than the person you were born and raised as. You are taking steps to recreate yourself.

Changing your worldview doesn't happen overnight. The entirety of your life experiences has created how you see the world as well as many cognitive habits. Transforming takes time and effort.

Although my formative experiences didn't set me up with a negative worldview, I still unwittingly engaged in changing my worldview through my poetry, songwriting, philosophical studies, and contemplative thought. I wouldn't consider the changes to be drastic, but changing your worldview in any way is a substantial feat of psychological control. I hope my experience with this can help you, too.

Disclaimer

I'm not a psychologist or philosopher, but I have spent

decades learning to maintain what I think is a healthy outlook on life, including my self-image. Being a songwriter and erstwhile poet, I've put a lot of thought into these ideas. Most were gleaned from other sources, but a few are mine, or at least I conjured them before I read them elsewhere.

I have made every attempt to provide information that is accurate and complete, but this book is not intended as a substitute for professional medical or psychological advice. This book is not meant to be used, nor should it be used, to diagnose or treat any medical or psychological condition. Readers are advised to consult their medical advisors whose responsibility it is to determine the condition of, and best treatment for, the reader.

I don't expect that this book will become anyone's one-stop shop for advice. It's a work in progress and always will be. I'm just offering it up in hopes that bits and pieces will find some usefulness for you. It is my recommendation that the reader uses ideas that currently make sense to them, and revisit the rest from time to time.

A Seminal Moment

People sometimes say when you overly react to someone else's opinion or actions that you've "given them control" over you. For example, one of the seminal moments in my life was in my 20s. I was driving home when a guy in a pickup truck passed me and flipped me off. I really had no idea why and it pissed me off. About 30 minutes after arriving home, I found myself still stewing on the incident. What did I do? What the hell was wrong with that guy? I wanted to hunt him down and confront him. Then it hit me. I had lost 30 minutes of my life because I let this guy have control over me. And it wasn't just 30 minutes wasted. It was 30 minutes of anxiety. It was 30 minutes of resentment. 30 minutes of suffering. And for what? It was pointless. I learned that, first, I didn't even know that guy, so why should I care? I didn't do anything wrong as far as I knew, and certainly not intentionally. If he was upset, that was his problem, not mine. Second, I learned I needed to do a better job of staying in the moment instead of stewing on past events. And if I was really good at the second part, I would've recognized the first part a lot quicker and short-circuited the whole thing.

That was big for me. Being in the moment. Validating my own perspective, but not at the total expense of everyone else's. It's not a zero-sum game, it's a balancing act. If I had known that guy, we would've probably argued about it and hopefully come to a mutual understanding, but I didn't, so I eventually let it go. His problem, not mine. The key was valuing my own opinion and being present enough to see that's what I needed to do.

Unbeknownst to me, I was discovering Stoicism and learning to practice mindfulness. I've had a few of these seminal moments in my life, the result of a lot of self-examination and acceptance. For many years I've been discovering and practicing what's in this book. I now view this episode as the pivotal moment when I started to find the control to live a content life.

Rethinking My Perspective

As long as I can remember, I felt slightly like a nonconformist. Like many kids, I felt different, but I valued that and wasn't afraid to pursue the path less traveled. This manifested itself in many ways but most significantly it eventually prompted a wholesale change in my worldview.

Shortly after high school, I was away at college surrounded by new things and people. I had a wonderful childhood and had no ostensible reason to eschew the cultural construct I was raised in. Still, I had this feeling that I wasn't myself yet. I knew that my perspective wasn't something I helped to create. I made a decision that would ultimately give me much greater control over my sense of well-being. I began to reshape my personal perspective. I began to change the way I see the world.

I took a bit of a dramatic step and tried to mentally wipe the cultural slate of my past clean. All beliefs, values, and assumptions came into question. I wanted to start from scratch. Later I realized that completely disassociating from your past isn't possible, but the effort allowed me to accept that there were many, many things I didn't know. I had to accept my ignorance.

I also started making efforts to build a philosophy that I could call my own, which meant asking and trying to answer a lot of questions. This required a lot of curiosity.

I started reading books on different philosophies and came to the conclusion that mindfulness, or living in the moment, was one of the important ways to maintain contentment. In my own observations of nature, I concluded that balance is an important aspect of living, which was also mentioned in some of the books I was reading.

I took the assorted parts that made sense to me and started using them. Accepting ignorance, being curious, mindful living, and striving for balance were important keys I discovered. Throughout this time I was writing. I had moved away from poetry and was starting to find my way as a songwriter. As is repeatedly mentioned during this book, I think any sort of writing is an important way to get traction in the process of self-understanding and make cognitive changes to be the person you want to be.

The result of this process wasn't the conclusion of a philosophical construct of deep truths, but more of a guide to keep me well on my journey. A set of tools to help maintain my contentment from moment to moment. It is this book. Like myself, it will evolve with later editions.

INTRODUCTION

Who Am I and Why Did I Write This Book?

I am a father, musician, songwriter, wine salesman, photographer, poet, author, and occasional philosopher focusing on the pragmatic. While I haven't pursued a formal education on the matters in this book, I will say that I have a lot of experience in being in control of my own contentment. I've had a lifetime of good teachers and experiences, engaged in lots of analysis, and done a fair amount of studying of religions and philosophies, as well as psychology. My journey as a songwriter and poet is one primarily of self-discovery and, later, self-acceptance. My view has been informed by books like Jonathan Livingston Seagull, What the Buddha Taught, Meditations, Zen and The Art of Motorcycle Maintenance, The Prophet, Crito and The Death of Socrates, The Tao of Pooh, American Dreamer, and Atlas Shrugged. I also listen to the Hidden Brain podcast for insights on psychology. Most importantly, my parents gave me the latitude to grow into myself, allowing me to make my own decisions (often known as "mistakes") while providing guidance and lessons that often took me years to recognize as such.

Please understand that when I use the word "informed" it also refers to some of the things I've read and observed that taught me how not to be. I don't regard any of these previously mentioned reference materials as a Bible. Furthermore, my adherence to pragmatism does not accommodate idealism, as ideals are unattainable. Therefore, theology doesn't hold much interest for me, outside of the usefulness of any given lesson gleaned from it. I liken ideals to stars in the sky–they are good for providing direction, but we must realize that we can't actually reach them. We need to balance the need to strive for an ideal with the reality that it is not attainable. There is no honor lost in failing to reach an ideal. In fact, there is no honor lost in failing, period. That we tried and failed at anything is simply being human and an opportunity to learn.

We have to try.

The vast majority of real-world solutions occupy complex gray areas, where, if you are honest about your ignorance, the questions are easy and the answers are not. Oftentimes, multiple solutions that need to work together simultaneously, and even then, they might not provide total satisfaction.

When I started writing this book, the intent was simply to give something to my children for guidance as they go through life's ups and downs. Soon after, a friend mentioned that they would like to read it and others might, too, so why not write a book? It is my best hope that something in these pages might give you the notion to see the world and yourself a little bit differently and give you some new tools for gaining more control over your well-being. I am also eager to hear feedback from your perspective, about what works for you and what doesn't, whether it's in these pages or not.

I also fully expect that after I finish this book, I will later regret some things said or unsaid as I grow and gain a greater perspective on myself and the world around me. However, I'm not one to let perfection be the enemy of progress, so I'll do my best and we'll see what happens.

This Book Does Not Represent An Ideology

This book does not attempt to construct an ideal. This book is simply a collection of tools, perspectives, and ideas that have helped me stay in control of my contentment, and I hope some of them can help you, too. I've tried to be thorough in my consideration of what they are and how they should be presented, but I encourage questions and challenges.

Although I don't subscribe to any religion or particular philosophical school of thought, that doesn't mean that I don't respect what they can offer to some people. But this book is exclusively about practical applications and putting faith in yourself, rather than elsewhere. Perhaps that isn't a great idea for everyone, or maybe it is. I don't know. I've found that most people want to be trusted, and putting faith in them tends to engender their own success and foster better relationships. I think the same results can be achieved by putting some faith in yourself.

How To Use This Book

This compilation of ideas, quotes, and tools took decades for me to accumulate. I didn't follow a linear path to self-acceptance as this book, or any book, inherently suggests by putting page after page. We all need different things at different times in our lives. Focus on the parts that hold the most usefulness to you now. It's a reference guide, so come back to it periodically to see how your perspective has changed and if anything else has become more relevant or interesting to you.

The Power Of Writing

I think writing down your thoughts, whether in a journal, a diary, a blog, a book, poetry, or song, is far and away the best practice to facilitate the changes in cognitive habits and psychological perspective needed to acquire the control needed to improve one's mental health. Not only does it provide a record against which you can gauge your personal development, but the very act of writing strengthens comprehension and memory.

Other practices also help such as meditation, mantras, mental exercises, and contemplative thought, but writing is the most powerful way to condition your brain. You may find a combination of different practices optimal. Find what suits you and do a little every day.

This book explores a lot of topics, but two activities in particular require daily time and consideration to achieve. 1) Developing a healthier worldview. 2) Developing your own self-image. These are significant undertakings. What we are talking about is changing our realities–how we see ourselves and the world along with the associated cognitive habits that we've developed over the years. Writing is such a powerful tool, I'm not sure that such dramatic changes can occur without it.

One of the key aspects of writing for personal development is that it provides an account of your perspective by which you can gauge your evolution. It's extremely helpful to be able to review something you wrote in the past and feel differently about it than when you wrote it. When I was writing my way through a hard time, I would regularly revisit what I wrote the previous month, week, or even day. It was often the case that I felt differently reading my words than when I first wrote them. When you're feeling down, this is a huge sign of hope that you aren't completely stuck. Even slight movement is encouraging.

Most importantly, writing with careful consideration helps bring your thoughts and feelings into greater focus. A greater understanding of what you think and feel, and why, will give you better and more insights as to ways to gain more control over your well-being.

I also think there is great self-acceptance in reading your own words. At first, it can feel awkward, but over time, you get used to it. It's like when you hear your voice recorded for the first time. Initially, it's very uncomfortable, but the more you hear it, the more you accept it. Getting comfortable reading your thoughts is a great step towards self-acceptance.

Even writing a list of things to do will not only help you remember and focus on what you need to do, but crossing out the tasks you've completed feels good!

I'll be revisiting the power of writing and other topics a few times in this book. I think it's important enough to reiterate, but I also want to make sure those who are hopscotching around this book are more likely to catch this.

INTRODUCTION

The Nutshell

If we need to learn contentment in this modern world, we have to learn to see things differently, including ourselves. We must also have as much self-knowledge as possible. We must accept that we have substantial ignorance, particularly regarding other people's thoughts about us. We must learn what we can control and how to control it, namely, our actions and reactions. We must accept the things we can't control, particularly other's actions and reactions. Curiosity plays a great role in self-understanding and being in the moment. Gratitude enhances our relationships with people and the world around us. Overall, we need a greater perspective that is neither positive nor negative, but simply broader and more accurate.

Part of being at peace is keeping a realistic perspective on yourself and your place in the world. With that in mind, I think we need to take a harder look at the big picture. I believe that the rising rates of loneliness, mental illness, suicide, and political divisiveness can be attributed in large part to living in a modern world that we as a species haven't psychologically adapted to yet.

THE BIG PICTURE-
ADAPTING TO A
MODERN WORLD

OK, I admit it. I picked, "It's Human To Give A Shit" because "A Practical Guide To Living Well In The Modern World" doesn't catch the eye so much. Plus, it seems that so many books now are about how to not give a shit that some effort to restore balance was in order. Yes, we care about what others think. We are hardwired to do it. We go along with the group. We need connections. We also judge and fear. This is human nature conditioned by hundreds of thousands of years evolving in pre-industrial times. Now these survival skills need an update for the modern mass society and technology that we are facing.

<u>Psychological Evolution</u>

What follows are several considerations I think our species is challenged by in this very new, modern, poly-cultural mass society. The last 100 years are completely different from the first 3,000,000 years.

These recent changes in how we interact both individually and culturally have been so incredibly dramatic and so quick, that we must reframe and redefine our traditional survival tactics involving judgment, anger, and, particularly, fear. Anxiety is becoming more and more pervasive, often leading to depression and taking an enormous emotional and economic toll on individuals, families, and society as a whole.

Another concern is our brains' apparent incompatibility with a modern world of complex problems. This manifests itself in ineffectual solution bases such as absolutism, conspiracy theories, and false diametrics. Rather than develop critical thinking strategies to arrive at better, more nuanced, and practical solutions, we still have a tendency towards simplistic, idealistic approaches, perhaps because the path is easier or because we evolved in simpler times. Perhaps the simple answers of old are inadequate in this complex, modern age. Or maybe we're just getting spoiled and lazy. Or all of the above. Whatever it is, it needs to change.

In short, our psychology of survival needs to evolve.

Fear

Sensing fear is one of our evolutionary keys to survival. Fears drive us to make decisions to keep ourselves and our families safe, to keep food on the table and a roof over our heads. Those whose fears were misplaced or lacking often found themselves removed from the gene pool. The survivors were the ones who feared best and we are their decendants.

In the pre-modern era, most found security in groups. Like herd animals, it was not safe to stray too far from the pack. There was safety in numbers. However, for the vast majority of those living in our current world, particularly in the United States, the opportunity to think and live independently is far more viable than in millennia past. It is no longer as necessary to go along with the group to survive. Our traditional fears are out of place in a modern world where survival skills and risks are far different than at any other time in history and prehistory. For example, a steady diet of fast food is far more likely to harm us than a wild animal or a stranger that just moseyed into town, yet we tend to fear those ideas far more than a trip to get a quick burger.

Another reason our evolutionary sense of fear isn't compatible with modern times is that the likelihood of physical harm is far lower than in the pre-modern era. Modern medicine has reduced the prevalence and severity of sickness and extended life expectancy. Although wars still occur, the vast majority of us have lived our entire lives in peace. Modern democratic government, police forces, technology, and economic policies have meant far more individual security, both in an economic and physical sense. So what happens when the traditional sources of fear have all but disappeared on a day-to-day basis? Sometimes fear kicks in for lesser things or things that we simply imagine or expect, even though they likely will never materialize. Perhaps our brains, being conditioned to fear harm for millions of years, are simply filling the void.

Without serious threats to our own physical health, much smaller or imagined fears can seem larger. This is why people who are regularly exposed to serious physical threats, like police officers, firefighters, and first responders, typically don't have "regular" anxieties, like social disorders, fear of heights, fear of public speaking, and other phobias. These problems seem trivial compared to the things they see at work on a regular basis. Unfortunately, because of their line of work, PTSD is a more common problem.

I think another reason modern humans tend to worry about more minor concerns is that we simply have more time on our hands. In the pre-modern era, humans spent far more time staying busy just to survive. There was far less time to be mired in thought, letting speculation, assumptions, and regret take root and take over our psyches. We were hunting, foraging, making things, and on the lookout for danger, not stewing over a co-worker's ambiguous comment, paying the bills, or worried about something we saw on the news or social media.

An additional concern, with the advent of mass media, is that fear is less a survival tool and has instead become an industry tool for profit and driving voters to the polls. People tune into bad news because we are hardwired to do so. Ratings go up which drives ad revenue. A "news" network may focus on doom and gloom events like shootings, accidents, and partisan political vitriol a majority of the time, but does that accurately reflect reality, and specifically, your reality? No, it almost certainly doesn't. I'd hazard a guess that virtually nobody faces these things the majority of the time on a normal day. This is just one of many reasons not to watch too much TV or online content and, instead, start tuning into boring, information-based news instead of commentary-based "news". Or maybe just watch less TV, period.

We also can reduce our fears by educating ourselves on the things we are fearing. For example, if you have a fear of snakes, you can study which snakes are venomous, which ones are more aggressive, what their habitat is, and techniques to avoid them. If you fear sending your kids to school because of all the mass shootings you see on TV, you could study and learn that the statistical likelihood of that happening is incredibly small. It may not eliminate the fear, but pursuing knowledge can help you put the fear into its proper perspective.

Cultural Identities And Adapting To A Polycultural Society

Because of exponential advances in communications, transit, and world population growth in the last 100 years, we have transitioned from more isolated, lower-density, regional monocultures to one big, high-density polyculture. Is this a good or a bad thing? I don't know. It doesn't matter because it's happened, so we have to work with it. While it may be sad to see some cultures disappear or otherwise blend into a new culture, nothing is permanent and there is plenty we can do to keep some of our formerly regional culture traditions going while respecting those of others.

I think one of the major problems in adapting to this new

melting pot of cultures is that many of us rely too strongly on our culture and cultural history to form our own identities. The problem is actually two-fold, one for the individual, one for society.

On the individual level, building your self-identity primarily on your cultural heritage potentially robs the individual of really discovering themselves. This isn't to say that cultural history shouldn't be important to one's identity, but to do it at the expense of individualism is a recipe for potential unhappiness and cultural conflict. Cultures produce a natural pressure to conform. People are hard-wired to go along with the crowd. Is following the group always the right decision? Of course not.

Also on a similar personal level, I think there's potential for the pride in one's cultural heritage to inhibit personal development. If we place too much importance on the deeds of our predecessors, that might lessen our desire to nurture our personal development. Of course, we can also be inspired by our cultural heritage. If we nurture our personal growth, informed by our cultural heritage, then that culture does not die, it is just evolving.

On the social level, a self-identity built primarily on personal cultural heritage can produce incredibly socially divisive results. If your identity is overly comprised of your cultural heritage, what happens when you meet someone that doesn't share that heritage? There's at least a chance that one or both of you don't approve of the other's heritage. At best, it's hard to relate and have a functioning relationship, at worst, conflict can ensue. Even genocides have occurred because of cultural differences. Why do many people identify so strongly with their cultural heritage? Is it logical to take praise for the accomplishments or blame for the mistakes of your ancestors? Their actions were their actions, not yours. A solid self-image not so deeply rooted in personal cultural heritage allows for the individual to be secure in themselves, without the dependence on cultural heritage. The result can be a greater tolerance and understanding of other cultures, as well as a greater sense of personal agency or self-ownership.

Another social aspect of cultural identities and polyculturalism is the subject of cultural appropriation. This happens when someone from one culture starts practicing the ways of another culture. This could be a style of music, speaking, dressing, cuisine, or even religion. I think most people don't consider this offensive and might, in fact, be flattered, but those who are linked very closely with their cultural background can get upset when someone not from their group adopts their ways. This seems especially likely when the person doing the "appropriating" is finding financial success in doing so. While some might cry "exploitation", I don't think that is giving much benefit of the doubt. If someone's passion for a cultural style propels them to great success, that is deserving of respect and appreciation. Rather than creating division, I'd hope inclusion would prevail. None of us started this life as a person we chose to be. If our efforts to recreate ourselves take us into a different cultural sphere, so be it. Respecting autonomy has to be a priority in a polycultural society.

To be clear, I don't think personal pride in cultural heritage is inherently bad–only when it supplants personal self-discovery and acceptance or leverages division between cultures. And there is some irony to the potential outcome where individuals in one, big polycultural world show more individuality than the people who cling to a group identity, fearing the loss of their culture and therefore, their "individuality" to some new "world order".

Transitioning From Honor Culture to Dignity Culture

I believe an important frame of reference for current social changes is the idea that we are transitioning from an Honor Culture to a Dignity Culture. There are probably entire books dedicated to this, but I'll sum it up as best as I can.

Before the technological revolution of the past hundred years or so, many places suffered from economic uncertainty and insufficient law enforcement. As a survival strategy, Honor Cultures were born. Honor Cultures feature the importance of reputation, group conformity, loyalty, and judgment. In lieu of adequate law enforcement, a reputation for being tough, dangerous, and vengeful could help protect you and your family from human predators who want to steal from you or otherwise harm you, your family, or your community. And by conforming to group values and being loyal, the group would help protect you, as well.

Honor cultures negatively impact our current society in multiple ways. First, they foster division. The group is paramount. Because there's an "us", there has to be a "them". "If you are not with us, you're against us."

Second, because honor culture requires mandatory group conformity, individual worth is not self-determined, it is defined by the group.

Third, as was referenced in the previous section, the potential for conflict escalates because of a strong cultural identity. Because the group's identity essentially destroys individuality within the group, all group members have conformed to the group identity. So when an outside person or group shows up that looks different, or says something that's considered culturally unacceptable, then conflict usually arises.

Additionally, because one's identity and self-worth are defined by the group, the punishment for not honoring the group and its dictates is being isolated or expelled from the group. Historically, this would mean anything from being shamed to being banished to being executed.

There are a host of other impacts, as well, such as group-defined gender roles, the breeding of mistrust, and the normalization of violence leading to elevated rates of domestic violence, murder, and suicide in our modern culture.

On the other end of the spectrum, we have Dignity Cultures, where individualism is accepted, conformity is not required, and one's worth as a person is considered inherent and self-determined. This is the culture of the modern era. With modern economic security and law enforcement, honor culture strategy is no longer necessary, yet the practice continues, even in many parts of the United States.

Honor and loyalty tend to have positive connotations, but in the context of Honor Culture, they are outdated tools that are now more destructive than constructive. While in the pre-industrial revolution era they may have been a good way to protect your family's physical and economic security, now all that lingers are the negative effects of divisiveness, violence, conformity, and shame.

Through this lens of Honor and Dignity cultures, we can see one very clear way how our current growing problems with anxiety and depression have been fueled. We're dealing with the residue of the Honor Culture's social determinant of one's self-worth. On the other side of the coin, it may be that human psychology and society haven't evolved enough to easily facilitate individual self-worth determination. To put it simply, self-determination of worth is a new concept for the masses. It's a new skill to learn. It's unsurprising that we still care far too much about what others think as we struggle with self-identity and self-esteem.

Absolutism

Another residual effect of Honor Culture is a mentality of absolutism. Because Honor Culture requires group conformity, there is little tolerance for a difference of opinion. This substantially restricts debate, innovation, compromise, and, ultimately, social and individual progress. In the consideration of social dynamics and individual development, all nuance is ignored and often loathed. It's us vs. them. "You're either with us or against us". "We're right, you're wrong". There is no sympathy, humility, or deference.

There are other reasons for this absolutism. One is the repeal of the Fairness Doctrine (requiring contrasting viewpoints to be presented on the news) spawning the proliferation of extremist politics on radio and TV. Our history and prehistory with monocultures is likely another. I'd imagine there's less of a desire for opposing viewpoints in a monoculture. Perhaps there is simply something about the human condition that fosters it. I imagine all these factors and others have contributing roles.

All this results in our western culture's predilection for diametric viewpoints. We tend to think in terms of polar opposites–black and white, good and evil, liberal and conservative--and disregard the fact that reality occupies the space in-between.

And absolutism can do serious damage when applied to self-image. In the case of someone suffering from mental illness, that person very well might blame themselves entirely for regretful behavior, when in reality the causes were born of conditions out of their control, such as genetics and cultural upbringing. The negative self-talk makes recovery that much harder, and the negative feedback loop becomes a vicious cycle. A more balanced perspective would allow a better understanding of the causes of the condition and what parts they do and do not control.

There is no practical application of absolutism that serves any good, either individually or communally, in my view. Beyond the fact that our problems of modern life rarely have simple solutions, absolutism squashes the opportunity for debate, learning, and compromise. In short, absolutism is for dictatorships, not democracies.

Causes And Symptoms

One thing I've noticed in our modern world is our tendency to want quick fixes. It's understandable. Quick fixes are cheaper, easier and we feel like we're doing something, but they rarely seem to work.

I believe this is a problem of addressing symptoms instead of causes. Sure, it's easy enough to take some acetaminophen when you have a headache. But if you keep getting headaches, wouldn't you like to know why, so you could prevent them in the first place? Maybe you're not hydrating enough. Perhaps you're eating too much sugar. Or you could have a brain tumor! National problems like environmental degradation, housing affordability, racial/gender inequities, unaffordable higher education, deteriorating international relations, insufficient healthcare, poor care for veterans, and houselessness are complicated problems that require much more than bandaids. Throwing money at the symptoms is not a complete strategy.

We seem to lack the wisdom, patience, discipline, and social concern to root out the causes and compromise on the complex solutions that require not just the money, but the time and sacrifices necessary to put forward a better future for young U.S. citizens and humans worldwide.

Often, I think the causes are, to a large degree, rooted in our cultural priorities. As it seems, social norms and cultural values change relatively slowly, but they do change. What follows are a couple of examples where some changes might show huge benefits to humankind.

<u>Cultural Priorities–The Almighty Dollar And Materialism</u>

There is no doubt that materialism has benefited humankind, although in mostly unintended ways, I would argue. The desire for personal gain has fueled a lot of innovation and improved the quality of life for the vast majority of humankind. And on a fundamental level, we all need a certain amount of stuff to survive–things that are acquired through productivity. So the desire for personal gain has inherent benefits both individually and socially.

Currently in the United States, the wealthiest country in the world, the Almighty Dollar is effectively our religion. All other priorities, including human well-being, are a distant second.

Our desire for more has also made us the most indebted country in the world. And how are we benefiting? Our environment is in shambles. Affordable housing is almost non-existent. Health care, especially mental health care, is not affordable, widely available, timely, and of the quality expected in the wealthiest country in the world. We are striving for more, but in many important ways, we're getting less.

In many places in the United States, the average household income ($75,000 in 2022) is not enough to keep up with expenses. In fact, there is ample evidence that nearly 50% of households with annual income of $100,000 are living paycheck-to-paycheck.

There are two sides of this coin. One, as previously mentioned, is the rising cost of essentials like housing, food, and medicine. The other is what we consider "getting by". Is it living in a 3,000sf home? Is it driving an $80,000 car? Is it having a beach house or yacht? Is it having a $250,000 RV that also is costly to operate?

I'm not here to judge, but when we start to rely on material gain and wealth to achieve some level of happiness, it becomes, to put it mildly, highly inefficient. More individual wealth does not directly correlate to being proportionally more happy. It also can damage society by helping to fuel inequity and economic insecurity.

Once we get our basics for survival covered, the heavy lifting for establishing contentment is done, at least in the financial sense. Adding more and more wealth doesn't create, proportionally, more happiness, studies show. It becomes more and more wasted.

The scarcity factor is also at play. Desirable things get

more valuable with scarcity. As you become more wealthy, scarcity becomes, well, more scarce. So appreciation and gratitude for those things start to decline. In short, we start taking for granted the things we used to appreciate more when we could less afford them.

All this is not to discount the presence and impact of philanthropy in the US and elsewhere, but the scales need more balancing. Investing your surplus wealth in other, more needy, parts of your community would not only establish a better and safer community but also be more rewarding than living in that oversized, luxury home. Not to mention how downsizing would help make the housing market more affordable, as well.

Lastly, making more efforts to help others less fortunate isn't just being kind, it provides greater security to all of us. The primary reason people steal is because they are either trying to survive or trying to be rich. If our cultural priorities didn't glorify wealth, then much of this insecurity would disappear. This concept also applies to neighboring countries. For example, in the 20th century, if the U.S. had more substantial partnerships with Central and South American countries to help develop economic security, then immigration to the US, illegal or otherwise, would likely be at a more manageable level because people wouldn't be fleeing their home countries as much. This is also another example of addressing symptoms instead of causes.

<u>Cultural Priorities–Sports, Entertainment And Other Stuff</u>

I think most of us agree that we'd like to see more equitable wealth distribution. Why don't we offer more pay for teachers, social workers, counselors, and police ? In our mostly capitalist society, people get paid what the market dictates, so what people earn is largely determined by their value to society. That sounds fine, but when teachers have to scrape by and take second and third jobs while famous athletes, coaches, actors, and musicians make multi-millions, even billions, I would say that our cultural values are askew.

I'm not suggesting we don't need these forms of entertainment, or that those who do those jobs shouldn't be handsomely paid, but I do think our oversized interest in them reflects a very imbalanced set of priorities.

Part of the problem may lie in the idea that we generally spend more time and money distracting ourselves from our problems than actually dealing with them.

We all need some entertainment, healthy distractions, and a community of people we share interests with, but we also need a society where those who maintain and nurture the well-being of its members are also adequately compensated so they can focus their work and families knowing their future is secure and without being distracted by financial difficulties, second jobs and the stresses they bring. Additionally, many of these career fields are inadequately filled for the societal need. We need more and better teachers, mental health counselors, and social workers which greater compensation and higher social regard will attract.

The result would greatly increase the quality of life for all of us.

Modern Communication Issues

As I see it, the biggest problem with modern, personal communication like texts, DM's, and emails is that without seeing somebody, you miss all their non-verbal cues such as voice inflection, facial expressions, body language, and eye language. Without these non-verbal cues, verbiage is ripe for miscommunication, especially in an era where messages are so short and to the point. For example, these days it is common for many folks to say "Shut up!" when they are surprised or excited. If you received this in a text, without non-verbal cues, you might take this the wrong way. Or maybe the context of the conversation makes it clear that they are excited, but you misinterpret why they are excited. Maybe you said you wanted to cook for them, and they are excited to see you and try your food, but you take it to mean that they are simply surprised you even know how to cook, and you take offense.

In days long gone by, people took the time and effort to more comprehensively explain their thoughts and feelings in letters that were far more lengthy than your typical text or Twitter post. Consequently, people today generally have a less thorough understanding of their thoughts and feelings. Self-understanding suffers. Relationships suffer.

Meanwhile, schools have reduced free play to a brief after-thought, minimizing the importance of the social, communicative, and cognitive skills developed when kids are allowed to be on their own, including learning how to read each other's non-verbal cues and build relationships. Throw into the mix kids staring at smartphones instead of each other and you have a mix of circumstances that is promoting poor communication skills across generations. The result is poorer and fewer relationships. This is one of the reasons for the rising rates of loneliness, depression, and anxiety.

Helicopter Parenting And Micromanaged Schools

Another source of elevated stress and anxiety is the result of parents not giving children enough freedom to develop self-direction, social skills, and risk assessment. Kids can't raise themselves, but they still need to develop autonomy and confidence. The need to take chances and succeed or fail and get up and try again. They need to climb trees, ride their bikes around the neighborhood, meet other kids, and explore. However, more and more parents hover over their children constantly in an attempt to give their them the safest, risk-free childhood possible.

Meanwhile, at school, nearly every minute of the day is micromanaged by the teachers, who are micromanaged by the state legislators. If the kids are lucky, they may get 30 minutes of true, free-play recess. Even then, it's not enough.

Of course, we should intervene if we see a child making a potentially life-altering mistake, but 99% of the time, whether it's falling off the jungle gym, getting a bad grade, or eating too much candy on Halloween, they'll recover and be better for it.

So children are losing their opportunities to develop confidence, self-direction, and risk assessment. They grow up to be anxiety-ridden adults because they've had virtually no experience making their own decisions. Fear of driving, meeting new people, or trying new things leads to isolation and depression. Then, many turn to social media, which, of course, compounds the problem.

Phones And Social Media

I hope by now we're all aware of the inherent problems with smartphones and social media. They undermine our ability to connect with our immediate surroundings, effectively removing us from the moment entirely. They also distort our self-image through a sea of virtual eyes, likes, and short comments, all of which are ripe for miscommunication. A simple "like" gives us a little dose of dopamine, not unlike what drugs, alcohol, and gambling do, making it potentially highly addictive. Additionally, there is the non-stop barrage of manipulation and distortion through ads, sensationalized "news" and political feedback chambers.

Do you control it, or does it control you?

Culture Wars

As previously stated, when our identity is too closely linked with our cultural heritage, we run the risk of being unable to tolerate people with other cultural norms. We can feel that our way of life is threatened or that our way of life is simply correct and that others need to change to live the way we do. This can threaten our friendships, familial relations, and group interactions and even be used as a weapon by politicians and hucksters.

We all grow up indoctrinated into a culture of some sort to some degree, so it's understandable that we sometimes feel inextricably a part of something, and that it is a part of us. But at some point, we must become more of our own person, and make some practical decisions to improve and maintain our contentment. Shedding less constructive elements of our culture and adopting new, more constructive ones will not only improve your life, but also give you more ownership over your sense of self. Knowing that you had the freedom to decide and make changes on your own behalf instead of being indoctrinated or forced into a cultural construct is largely what dignity is all about.

Similarly, we must also recognize that any given culture is not permanent. Cultural signifiers such as music, food, art, and language are constantly changing. So, too, do cultural values. While it may be sad to see a certain way of life disappear, we can still strive to keep the best parts and carry those forward into our ever-changing world.

Education

I believe that public education is one of the major reasons for economic prosperity in the United States. I also believe that human evolutionary psychology doesn't equip us for the social pressures that occur in our modern schools. My theory is that for hundreds of thousands of years, children were always subordinate members of a family or tribe. They never needed to deal with the pressures that come with being in a large group of peers. Only in the last 150 years have young people been placed into schools where, for the first time in human history, they have their own culture. Given this happens during the formative stages of a person's development, it is little wonder that so many kids have a hard time with their self-esteem during this time.

In recent decades, many efforts have been made to address this, like having in-school counselors, teacher awareness training, and updated teaching techniques. These are great steps, but we need to commit more resources to them. Current funding levels reflect our country's lack of commitment to mental health care. There is still a lot more we can do to help our kids not be psychologically debilitated, so they don't grow up having to unlearn how to be down on themselves. We can do a better job as adults setting a better example of promoting personal development and social and political cooperation.

Climate Change

Climate change poses an incredible challenge to humanity, and also to many of us as individuals. While humanity is challenged to work together to manage this issue, individually we are not only challenged to make efforts that seem miniscule on a global scale, but many of us have to battle the stress and anxiety of our most feared speculative future outcome.

So many aspects of this issue embody many of the important topics covered in this book. Even though we may never see the results of our efforts, we have to try. We have to accept our ignorance that we don't truly know the extent of impending climate change nor the exact causes of it. We have to put our speculative assumptions about the future aside and focus on the here and now. We have to be curious and compromise to find solutions. We are going to have to change our habits. We are going to have to accept some things we cannot change while changing things we know we can.

As much as any event in history, how we handle climate change will define humanity for all future generations.

<u>Political Correctness</u>

Let's set the record straight. Everyone is politically correct for their own politics. The term only became weaponized after some folks didn't like the idea of being politically correct for someone else's politics.

When we meet our neighbors, co-workers, service industry workers, and even strangers, are we assholes? Do we deliberately push people's buttons? Do we let our unfiltered thoughts fly? Do we show total disregard for their wants, needs, and feelings? Of course not. We try to be nice. Whether you are empathetic or not, you can attract more flies with honey than vinegar. It is the politically correct thing to do.

Yet when certain people ask for their identities to be respected by way of preferred terminology or general consideration, that often seems to be a problem for some others.

I think this all ties into the earlier points of how we're still adapting to a highly polycultural society while simultaneously transitioning from Honor Culture to Dignity Culture. Many of us don't know how to accept those who are different from ourselves and our culture. It's us against them and they need to know who's boss.

It seems that those who don't have self-determined self-worth often don't respect those that do. The consequences of not evolving are not as dire as they used to be.

CONTENTMENT

Why "Contentment" And Not "Happiness"?

As I mentioned previously, I'm not sure that constant happiness is a realistic, or even healthy, goal. Research shows that constant efforts to be happy have the opposite effect. When that moment of happiness doesn't last, we struggle and toil to recreate a similar moment that also doesn't last or meet expectations. On top of that, achieving the sort of financial success that allows us to purchase all the things and experiences that we think will make us happy also fails as we quickly start to take those things for granted.

Contentment needs to be the baseline, the place we rebound to between the peaks and valleys of life.

Things That Block Contentment

It's human nature that negative experiences carry more weight than positive ones. For example, when I was a kid I was a football fanatic for my home team. I remember the pain of the losses being stronger and lingering longer than the joy of the victories. Another example is how people are far more apt to complain than compliment. If someone has a bad restaurant experience, they will tell 10 people. If they have a good experience, they might tell two. Modern research bears this out in that it is estimated that negative experiences carry

5 times the emotional weight of positive ones. Therefore, it stands to reason that an important consideration in improving contentment is reducing negative experiences. And while eliminating all negative experiences isn't realistic, we absolutely can reduce them and learn to recover better and more quickly.

Making better decisions can set us up for more contentment, but mindfulness, or being in the moment, plays a big role in how much contentment we experience. Self-induced pain is the pain we experience in anticipation of a speculative negative future event or memory from a past negative event. Research proves that when we experience this type of anxiety it activates the part of the brain that also is activated by physical pain. If we change our perspective to live in the moment instead of the future or past, we can drastically reduce self-induced pain and improve our lives.

Negative assumptions are another form of self-induced pain. For example, if a neighbor is driving by and doesn't wave or smile at you, you might feel slighted. You might assume you said or did something wrong, or that someone told your neighbor something negative about you. This can get your whole day going in the wrong direction. But do you really know what they are thinking? Of course not. They could've been totally lost in thought, distracted by bad news, just notified about a problem at work, or dealing with their own mental health issues. Perhaps someone ignored them and now they're engaged in the same self-induced pain that you're now engaged in! Once we accept that we all carry incomplete knowledge and cannot read minds, these negative assumptions become neutralized.

Another thing that can block contentment is when we don't know and accept ourselves well enough to make good life decisions. When we make life decisions based on the views of others or society and not self-understanding, unhappiness usually follows. Section 5 of this book is dedicated to self-knowledge and acceptance.

Traumatic experiences block contentment in a more dramatic way. Some ideas in this book may assist in overcoming trauma, but it's best to seek help from a licensed psychologist and psychiatrist.

Get Out Of Your Head

There is no doubt that the majority of this book is about getting in your own head, but you can't stay there forever. You have to get out of your head and focus on other things and people, too. Doing the work suggested in this book is like getting under the hood of your car. Once you get the engine running better, it's time to go out and drive. Eventually, we'll probably have to get under the hood again, but with attentive maintenance, the repairs should be minimal.

Note that in the following list of 13 keys to contentment, about half are concepts involving self-talk and half are not. In particular, self-knowledge and acceptance require a lot of internal debate to achieve, but once achieved, require much less.

Not getting too wrapped up in your own thoughts is an important consideration. If you find yourself mentally mired in overthinking, it's time to get out of your head and focus on the world around you.

13 Keys To Learning And Maintaining Contentment

I consider these to be fundamental to living a content life. I don't know that all 13 are collectively necessary, but I think the more you have, the more content you'll be.

Also, practicing 1-4 will make the rest come more naturally.

Keys 1-7–Learning And Maintaining Contentment

1. Gratitude–For everything. From someone holding the door for you to the air you breathe.

2. Living in the moment–Planning for the future and learning from the past are important, but real living is here and now. Never stray too far or too long from the present. Keep expectations at bay, both positive and negative.

3. Curiosity–it helps you be present, solve and avoid problems, learn, be creative, be humble, build relationships, keep your problems in perspective, and recover from them.

4. Personal Agency/Self-Control–Own your state of mind. While others' actions certainly impact your life, you are responsible for your own mental and emotional well-being. You have control to make decisions in how you act and react. Conversely, you cannot hold yourself responsible for another's decisions in how they act and react.

5. Self-knowledge and acceptance–Knowing and accepting who we are (for better and worse) gives a starting point for growth, informs our decisions on personal development, and offers a degree of comfort and understanding that only we can give ourselves. It can also aid in not taking criticism personally, as well as fostering debate and compromise.

6. Acceptance of the world/others–Railing against things we cannot change is stressful, distracting and usually pointless. Accept that uncertainty is a part of life.

7. Balance–I think balance in many aspects of living is extremely important, but is different for different people at different times of their lives.

Keys 8-13–Maintaining Contentment

8. Healthy personal connections–Maintaining healthy relationships is one of the biggest keys to contentment.

9. Having direction–We need to be feeling purpose in our lives, work towards goals, and make progress helping ourselves and others.

10. Doing things (showing progress/accomplishments)– Whether big or small, they all function to give us a boost

of self-esteem.

11. Money–As my dad said, "It's not everything, but it's damned important". The way I put it–"Money can't buy you happiness, but it will buy you misery if that's all you can afford." You don't need a mansion, just get your basics covered and you've eliminated a lot of stress that can block contentment.

12. Physical activity–Getting up and moving is good for your body, which means it's good for your mind. Beyond the inherent benefits of exercise, your feet can move you into psychologically beneficial situations, like a walk in the woods, or biking through your community and talking with people.

13. Practice being alone with and without your thoughts–It's been said that "we're born alone and we die alone". And there are plenty of times in between that we'll be alone or feel alone, too. Accepting this and practicing it a bit goes a long way toward self-acceptance. Take a walk in the woods or a drive in the country. Sometimes, you need to take the time to think. Sometimes you need to quiet your thoughts.

Learning and Maintaining Contentment–Keys 1-7

1. Gratitude

What happens when you think to say "thank you", and then say it? First, it acknowledges a connection between you and whoever you're thanking. It also shows the other person that you appreciate that connection, that you appreciate them and what they did for you. Additionally, thanking them will likely give them a little boost of purpose–that their actions made a positive impact on your life. That brings them a sense of accomplishment, which brings a little contentment. This also helps to strengthen the connection. All this from a little gratitude.

Note that I said "think" to say "thank you". The watered-down effect of rotely saying "thank you" does not work the same way. People can tell when it's out of habit or when it's thoughtful. Just be grateful in the moment and it will show.

In general, being grateful brings a positive impact to your perspective on life. Life always has ups and downs, but if gratitude is a habit for you, the downs won't feel quite so down, and the ups will feel even higher.

If you were not lucky enough to be raised to be grateful, how do you get there? It's a habit, like anything else. But a cognitive habit is not one to change quickly. Be patient with yourself and approach it like chipping away at a boulder. Do a little bit every day and you will get there. Note when you aren't being grateful. Note when you are. Log a little of these things every day just to help remind yourself. Take an extra moment to write a short explanation of why you're grateful for each thing on your list.

You can also make a list of considerations of how your life would be less satisfactory if not for the things you should be grateful for. Revisit this list regularly and add to it. Even if your life isn't all you want it to be, the list is probably a lot longer than you think.

2. Living in the Moment

The modern term for this is mindfulness, but I feel that term has been overused and lost its impact. I prefer "being present" or "being aware". Most famously asserted in Zen Buddhism, it is the idea that there is no future and no past, there is only the present moment. If you are not being here and now, then you are not really living.

Being a pragmatist, I value the ability to ponder the past and the future. In memories of the past, we can find joy and wisdom, as we celebrate our experiences and learn from our mistakes. In looking to the future we can make plans and set goals. For some people, the past can be a source of pain, and the future, a source of anxiety. Whether positive or negative, we must always rebound to the present. The present is where we are free from the anxiety of overthinking and worries of the past, future, unknowns, and speculation, like "what ifs". It is clinically proven that such anxieties activate the part of the brain where we feel pain. So dwelling on the pain of the past is literally re-experiencing the pain. And worrying about a future that may not even come to pass is equally unnecessary. Learning to be in the moment helps to alleviate this self-inflicted pain. This is what is meant by, "pain is inevitable, suffering is optional". But if living in the moment is your default mode, you can essentially eliminate this kind of suffering.

Keep expectations at bay. Whether you have high hopes or expect the worst, it serves only to pull you away from the reality of what you need to do here and now. My sister reminded me of what I used to tell her, "Don't get attached to the outcome". Whether you are in high-stakes negotiations, trying to cultivate a relationship with someone, or simply trying to get a good night's rest, expectations only serve to distract you from the moment and put pressure on you that might adversely affect your performance. Stay focused on the here and now. The present is where things get done and contentment is found.

Children naturally live in the present, which is why they have a keener sense of joy and wonder and are more resilient than most adults. Sometimes I joke with my kids about how I'm never going to grow up completely, but there's definitely some truth to it!

Living in the moment is also critical in self-understanding, breaking undesirable habits, and creating desirable ones. When we are present in the moment, we are much more aware of the decisions that make up our tendencies and routines. It's in the moment that we can catch ourselves and say, "Is this the decision that's right for me?". Temporary things can become permanent over time, and if you are not present, you may eventually find yourself not being the person you intended to be when you were younger.

There are many techniques for developing mindfulness. Focusing on your breathing is a great one. Paying attention to your senses is another. What are you seeing, hearing, feeling, smelling, or maybe tasting? Even if you are sitting still, your senses are telling you things. Asking questions and being curious about your surroundings is also a good tool for being present, as well as getting out of your head. With practice, you will develop control of your thoughts and be able to turn them off or push them away when you want to.

3. Curiosity

Curiosity is an important tool to help us live in the moment, or maybe it's a result of living in the moment. Perhaps it's both. Curiosity doesn't happen without awareness. When you are living in the moment, you are naturally curious. And when you are curious, you are naturally living in the moment. This can be extremely helpful in a myriad of ways–solving problems, avoiding problems, learning, being creative, building/maintaining relationships, and more, not to mention expanding your self-understanding. All of which help in maintaining contentment.

Curiosity is a trait we all had as children, but it gets smothered under adult stresses and hubris. However, curiosity can be awakened when we acknowledge and accept all the ignorance that we all possess. We tend to think we know more than we actually do and oftentimes act like we know it all. But when we are being present and accepting the gaps in our knowledge then our curiosity is set free. Accepting ignorance is covered more thoroughly in the section in this book called "Your Worldview". This ignorance is also a reminder of our small place in the world and the universe, helping us to stay humble, continue to learn, build better relationships, and keep our problems in perspective.

All these things–relationships, keeping problems in perspective, humility, learning, and self-acceptance–can help stave off depression. If you are curious, you will never be bored. If you are living in the moment, then you are paying attention. If you are paying attention, you will notice things that you would otherwise miss. These things will often make you think of more questions. That is curiosity.

Another benefit of curiosity is the role it can play in the aftermath of adversity. After a failure, loss, or trauma, it is natural for us to replay the event over and over. But playing a game of "what ifs" isn't really curiosity, it's simply regret, confusion, or self-reproach. True curiosity helps keep us in the moment, while simultaneously stepping outside ourselves to think of different ways to look at the problem. Being curious helps us not just understand, fix, and avoid the problem, it can also help us see how we're doing and what we need to do to continue to recover.

Being curious allows us the intellectual freedom to question even common knowledge, reassess our cultural upbringing, be open to new experiences, and calm our fears. In short, it fosters learning, growth, self-direction, and contentment.

4. Personal Agency/Self-Control

If you don't own your emotional/mental state 100% of the time, that means at some point, someone else does. This simply means don't give up control of your psychological well-being to someone else. When someone else's actions cause you to feel stress, anger, insecurity, or sorrow, you have a choice of how to react. Maybe they intended for you to feel that way, or maybe not. Either way, you must own your emotions, manage your reactions, and set about moving forward in a direction of your choosing. Letting your emotions get the best of you and losing control is always destructive. For many of us, it's going to happen sometimes. Hopefully, we can learn how to reduce the frequency.

Owning your mental and emotional well-being is about doing the daily things on your own to set yourself up to have good days. It's making decisions about your work, friends, family, recreation, physical health, and mental health that improve your life. For some of us, it comes easier, for others it's more challenging, requiring diligent and daily effort, planning, and persistence until it becomes second nature.

It's important to understand that you may have friends or family who pose obstacles to improving your mental health, yet you still care about them a great deal. Limiting your exposure to these people is likely necessary at times, but cutting them off permanently might not be best for your long-term well-being, either. If you need a break, it is absolutely okay to tell them you need a break.

A good analogy for this concept of personal agency is that it is better to be a mighty oak than a fallen leaf in the wind. Let's put our roots down so we have a firm grasp of who we are, who we want to be, and how to grow.

5. Self-Knowledge And Acceptance–"Who Am I?"

I believe that self-understanding and self-acceptance are fundamental to contentment. This means having an ongoing, honest look at yourself to understand your failures, successes, strengths, weaknesses, habits, idiosyncrasies, preferences, personality, etc. Your perspective of yourself, like everyone else's perspective of you, will always be inherently incomplete, and probably slightly flawed. But having a starting point to know yourself is essential. Only when we have a good picture of ourselves can we make better decisions that set us up for success, whatever success is to you. And your definition of success will probably change as you learn more about yourself.

Whether it's a career path, recreation, relationships, or spirituality, the decisions we make will bring us greater contentment if we have a better idea of who we are to start with.

Early in my twenties, I decided that if I was going to be my "true" self and lay claim to any sort of free will, then I needed to try to strip away the constructs that my culture had given me–from religion to politics to the food and music I preferred. I put "true" in quotation marks because I'm not sure that anyone can ever completely disassociate themselves from their origins and cultural constructs, but I did try. I conceptualized my ignorance and questioned everything that I was led to believe. It was a healthy exercise for me and gave me great insight into who and how I was at the time, as well as a much greater sense of agency. However, I eventually realized that we are always tied to our past. All of our choices and circumstances are forever informed by it, for better or worse. It's like wondering what our life would be like if we could go back in time and make different decisions. We can learn a lot from reflecting on it, but we can't spend much time and energy on it because then we're not really dealing with the here and now. We can't change the past. However, by putting our origins into a broader context, we can increase our understanding of ourselves and use it as a starting point as we move forward in the direction of our choosing.

A subtle, but important, aspect of self-acceptance is developing the ability to not take every bit of advice, criticism, or failures personally. I've spent most of my life in sales, so I realized early on that if I didn't learn to separate the business from the personal, my life was going to be a lot more difficult than it needed to be. Some refer to this as growing "thick skin", but I prefer to think of it simply as "business is business". We shouldn't be tying so much personal equity into our ideas or being "right". We are all eternally distant from perfect knowledge, so let's drop the pretenses and listen to what others have to say. Fight for the best resolution, not simply to win. And if you lose or fail in an endeavor, pick yourself up and learn from the experience.

Developing self-knowledge and acceptance is an important process covered later in Section 5.

6. Acceptance Of The World/Others

Before we can make attempts to change parts of the world around us, we must first accept them as they are, or at least as we see them.

I'm not sure how to expound on this as it seems pretty simple to me. However it does occur to me that accepting things as we see them might be a little easier when we realize that we only see the parts of the world we see. As I said before, our perspectives are inherently incomplete. For instance, if a person is short and curt with you, you may take offense or feel insecure because you think that they don't like you or you did something wrong. But you don't know what's going on in their head. Perhaps they suffer from a mental condition, are dwelling on past trauma, or are just having a bad day. If you feel reasonably sure that you didn't do or say anything wrong or were misunderstood, then it's best just to accept it, let it go, and move on. You might even check in with that person to see if they're ok.

Another important thing to accept is uncertainty. Uncertainty is just a part of the ignorance and incomplete view of reality we all possess. Whether it's other people's thoughts, what the future holds, or trying to understand past events, we must accept that there are parts we will never understand completely. We shouldn't "spin our wheels" on these things and instead move forward.

Ultimately we can only know what we know, build on that knowledge, and grow wiser. If we choose to encourage change in the world around us, we must be patient and persistent, with no expectations. Change comes slowly, especially when you are dealing with people. Acceptance of things we cannot change is also a part of Stoic philosophy, referenced in Section 6.

When it comes to accepting others, it's helpful to understand that no one chose to be born a certain way, or into a certain situation. We all start out as someone we did not choose to be. We are born with genetic predispositions and into families and communities not of our choosing. Later, after being raised in certain ways and living in a body we did not choose, hopefully we gain enough autonomy to work towards being the person we want to be. Recognizing this in others and yourself makes acceptance much easier. It also facilitates the forgiveness of others, which goes a long way in promoting contentment.

7. Balance

Balance is an important aspect of well-being. A position of balance is very subjective. What may be in balance for one person may not be for someone else or even for the same person at a different point in their lives.

Approaching aspects of your life with an unbalanced perspective can cause many problems. This might be an unbalanced approach to work/family where family connections suffer due to working a lot. Another example is where an extreme belief in an ideology might cause harm to yourself and your relationships, like dedicating yourself to an extreme partisan position in politics, giving no consideration for others' perspectives and values.

The various ways that balance affects living are outlined later in this book under "Philosophical Concepts That Make Sense To Me".

Maintaining Contentment–Keys 8-13

8. Healthy Personal Connections

It is well established that healthy personal connections; friendships, spouses, family, and community–are fundamental to emotional well-being. In fact, research shows that human connections are the most important part of your well-being–emotionally, psychologically, and even physically. The reason it is not at the top of my list is that I believe #1-7 are very important to building and maintaining healthy relationships.

The chemistry of relationships comes in various forms and different people need different things at different times in their lives. But ultimately, all relationships are a bit transactional, and both parties need to benefit for it to be an enduring relationship. I don't think this is something quantifiable, but suffice it to say that if either party feels like the relationship isn't benefiting them, or is detrimental to them, then they may feel the need to disconnect. The decision to disconnect permanently depends on the people involved. If it's someone you care a lot about or someone that you feel needs the help, then occasional contact may be appropriate, as long as you feel it won't harm you too much.

Scorekeeping in relationships is generally considered a bad thing. Yet, as I just mentioned, there is a transactional aspect of relationships that requires us to keep score to a degree. So where is the cut-off? Where does monitoring what's healthy in a relationship turn into a destructive habit of keeping score? Scorekeeping at its worst becomes food for anger and ego-centricity. It's when you do it so often that you develop the constant expectation that the other person is going to do the thing that's been causing you harm, and you live in constant anxiety. The other person has lost all benefit of the doubt. Trust is lost. At this point, you need to reexamine your cognitive habits–scorekeeping and negative expectations—and the relationship itself. Everybody is different and every relationship is different, so you must find the resolution between what you can control (the cognitive habit) and what you can't (the other person's behavior). Consider the level of commitment the relationship requires. Consider how the relationship is or is not benefiting you. Consider the thresholds of what can jeopardize your well-being. After considering these things, you need to communicate your feelings and what you want. These conversations can become emotional but try not to let emotions get the best of you. People can get very defensive in this situation, but if you present a thoughtful case of how you're feeling, they should be receptive to some compromise. If they aren't, then I'd suggest the relationship may no longer be mutually beneficial. Depending on the chemistry of the relationship and what the relationship requires, you can either accept this or not. Sometimes the path forward is simply the least worst option. Hopefully, it's more positive than that.

Speaking of chemistry, be aware of the defining nature of the relationship. For example, I know of situations where two friends were both dealing with a lot of problems, and their relationship became defined by complaining, validating, consoling, and counseling each other over past trauma and current struggles, almost as if they were each other's therapists. Ultimately, the weighty nature of their standard interactions was too much and one had to take a break from the relationship. They later reconnected and rebuilt the relationship, learning to keep discussions fun and lighter more often. A good friend is there to help you through a tough time, but most people need friendship also as a source of joy, not just drama.

Research also suggests that deep friendships aren't as critical to well-being as you might think. Even casual associations with neighbors, a crossing guard, a barista, co-workers, or customers can have a meaningful impact on your life.

9. Having Direction

A lot is said of having goals, and they are certainly important, but I think having purpose is equally or even more important. Sometimes a purpose leads to creating a goal. Examples would be finding purpose in gardening, then deciding to create a garden for your community, or pursuing being a master gardener or incorporating it into a career. Other times, the purpose is clear, but the goals aren't, such as caring for children or pets. There is no goal or finish line. The purpose is in the journey itself, which is actually very Zen, although it can be frustrating for some people to not be able to gauge their progress. Not only is this the case with raising kids, but also in gauging your personal growth. I think the key is to accept that sometimes there is no road map, and you just have to keep your feet moving and find your way. Being on the journey is being in the moment, and the moment is all we have.

On the subject of having a purpose, I'm not simply talking about some grand notion of your life's overall direction as you hear on the talk shows. It is equally important to have a purpose, or purposes, in smaller doses, even if they change from day to day. Purpose can be found in nearly all our daily activities–maintaining a residence, picking up a piece of trash, reusing an item that might have been thrown away, cooking a meal, earning a living, or even putting air in your tires. It can also mean taking steps to improve your physical and mental well-being.

A sense of purpose is entirely subjective. It is up to you. A purpose can be slowly cultivated from a hobby or work. It can be born from a life change like a shift in a career or caretaking for a loved one. Inspiration can come from anywhere and anyone. Knowing yourself and accepting yourself will make the focus even clearer. As it seems to be with so many things, being in the moment can facilitate well-being to a huge extent, including being aware enough to see when inspiration strikes you.

Sometimes we get a little stuck. We don't know what direction to go in. When this happens, you have to just pick a direction and get moving. The act of doing nothing is very likely to be more detrimental than going in the wrong direction. If it turns out to be the wrong direction, then you will have learned something. You can't steer a ship that isn't moving.

10. Doing Things

You would think this one would be obvious, but to me, it wasn't. I was actually around 40 before the light went on. I think it was after I had cleared a sink drain and, checking it after reassembly, I felt this curious satisfaction watching the water swirl easily down the drain. Mind you, I don't love clearing sink drains, cleaning the kitchen, power washing the patio, and many other chores, but work needs to be done and I still get a small dose of satisfaction looking at my finished work.

Small, daily accomplishments are important, but so are larger ones that take time, like weight loss, quitting smoking, or home projects. Philanthropic goals are also rewarding, like organizing a toy drive during the holidays, leading a clean up crew at a local park, fundraising for the PTA or building a scale model of the solar system at your daughter's elementary school (yeah, I did that, lol). In any case, when you are doing things to improve your or another's world, it's guaranteed to provide at least a little satisfaction and sense of accomplishment.

Accomplishments aside, just making progress can also give you satisfaction or at least provide a sense of movement that ensures you're not stagnating. When most of us were kids, we loved being measured to see our growth progress. Even though we stop physically growing, we can continue to grow emotionally and intellectually. Reading books, even occasionally, is great for this. I also think writing is also a great gauge for growth. Whether you're writing poems, prose, songs or a journal, it is very illuminating to periodically revisit things you've written months before because you almost certainly will notice that your perspective has changed. Not only does this shift remind me that I'm evolving, but it also forces me to think about the situation I was writing about, why I feel differently, and what I can learn from it.

11. Money

When I was an idealistic and slightly spoiled kid, I once told my dad "money isn't everything!" This was likely in response to a normal parental concern that pursuing a career as a rock and roll star might need a backup plan. He said, "Well, money isn't everything, but it's pretty damned important." Well, you know, it sure is. You cannot buy happiness, but you can certainly buy misery if that's all you can afford. This is a bit of hyperbole, of course. Some people have learned to have a positive outlook even in the most humble of living standards or dire circumstances, and there is tremendous value in that. And if I was single, it's possible that "money" wouldn't even make this list. However, having kids changed the equation for me. Regardless, I think that most would agree that maintaining contentment is easier when you don't have to wonder where your next meal is coming from.

Additionally, being able to support yourself and others builds confidence and self-esteem and reduces stress. Becoming wealthy could afford you the resources and time to invest in your community through donations of your money and work, all of which will make you feel better as a person and build the connections that we as humans inherently need.

12. Physical Wellness

The psychological benefits of regular exercise are well-established but less regarded are the psychological benefits of being outside, moving, and getting things done. Going on a walk in the woods will give you the benefits of "green therapy". Mowing the lawn is exercise, but it also gives a little feeling of accomplishment, or "doer therapy". Riding your bike around your neighborhood gives you the opportunity to talk to neighbors, giving you "social therapy". You also could find social therapy at the gym!

A healthy diet also plays a role in physical wellness, of course. A balanced diet of fruits, vegetables, whole grains and lean proteins can improve digestion, boost energy levels, improve mental focus, promote better sleep, and reduce inflamation. This includes limiting processed foods, excessive sugar and saturated fats. However, I would argue the occasional chocolate chip cookie offers some psychological benefits, as well!

13. Practice Being Alone With And Without Your Thoughts

Don't listen to your earbuds on every run. Turn off the music in the car once in a while. Turn off the TV in the house. You will learn to enjoy the quiet and the extra latitude it gives you to think your thoughts or turn off your thoughts.

A few of my most formative years were spent living in the country with no neighbors. This left me to entertain myself most of the time. This was in the 70s, so there was no social media, no smartphones, no video games, and no cable TV. We had 3 channels to choose from and not a lot for a kid to watch. We weren't far from town, so I was involved with things like organized baseball, Boy Scouts, and swim team. I also had great friends that I would hang out with. But from about age 4-10, I had a lot of days where I was more or less left to my own devices out in the country. I would jump my bike over logs, play with the dogs, throw a baseball against the fence, play with toys in the sandbox, and explore the woods. On rainy days I'd play with my Hot Wheels, draw, or read comic books. This was also the time when I started writing poetry and trying to figure out more about myself.

This time in my life was an early lesson in being on my

own. I think it conditioned me to not rely on others for entertainment, engagement, or validation. In many ways, it was one of the most important factors in my personal development and laid the foundation for my peace of mind as an adult. I think this sort of childhood is rare and becoming rarer, but there is no reason we can't engage in regular time alone to be with our thoughts, or without them.

Stress

Most of us have heard that stress kills. Scientists are still discovering ways that stress is harmful and potentially deadly. It can inhibit your immune system and contribute to high blood pressure, heart disease, weight gain, poor sleep, headaches, digestive issues, anxiety, depression, and probably other things we haven't discovered. This isn't to mention the potential for bad decision-making when stress distorts our judgment.

Learning contentment means less stress, which means better health, both physical and mental.

YOUR WORLDVIEW

What Is Your Worldview?

What is your worldview? Do you see the world as a safe or dangerous place? Do you see humanity as generally good or bad? Do you see the average person as trustworthy or not? Do you focus on the negative aspects of your life, history, and future, or the positive? Somewhere in-between? Do you notice failures far more than victories? Is the glass half-full or half-empty?

Some people seemingly have everything they could ever need and want, yet they are not happy. Then there are those who have very little and are very happy. You might have two people who have both suffered great losses and pain, yet one has maintained their optimism and gratitude while the other has nurtured only pessimism and resentment.

Somewhere in your formative years, through your childhood experiences, mentors' and peers' influences, cognitive habits, and perhaps some genetic predispositions, you start to see the world a certain way. Your worldview has a tremendous effect on your mental health. Not only does it paint the world a certain way, like "rose-colored" glasses, but it also colors how you see yourself. You are a part of the world, after all.

A worldview that employs pessimism, fear, condemnation, or distrust is only going to serve to erode your relationship with the world around you, including people. You might think you're fine with that, but you'd be wrong. Connections to other people are integral to good mental health. You don't have to be a socialite or the life of the party, but a good friend or three is nice to have.

Your worldview affects how you interpret others' actions and words, as well as your own. Therefore, it affects your relationships with others, and with yourself. It is very much what they mean by, "your perception is reality".

I would argue that an overly rosy worldview also carries some lesser pitfalls, but I think the greatest good would be in addressing those who are mired in chronic negativity.

The Vicious Cycle Of Self-Destruction

It's important to note how negative, self-destructive thoughts become a vicious cycle. If you have a worldview that fosters negative assumptions, those negative assumptions can damage your self-image and harm your relationships. As you become more isolated and depressed, this can serve to reinforce your negative assumptions about yourself and others, further entrenching your depression and isolation, which strengthens your negative assumptions, which deepens your depression and isolation, and on and on.

This shows how your perspective on the world is very much a self-fulfilling prophecy. How you see the world directly impacts your experience in it. So, if you want to break out of the cycle, you have to change your worldview and the cognitive habits that have rooted themselves into your brain over the years.

The goal here is not to develop a super-positive outlook. We want to achieve something more realistic and more constructive. We will need some exercises on positivity to achieve this, though. That is the direction opposite of negativity, after all.

Later in this section, I've included a suggested list of

mental exercises, but before that, we should note some other considerations.

Accepting Ignorance and Incomplete Perspective

"For I was conscious that I knew practically nothing..."
                                                    –Socrates

I believe that the first step towards changing your worldview is to accept your ignorance. Ignorance typically carries a negative connotation, but it shouldn't. We all have a ton of it and it's nothing to be ashamed of. In fact, it's pretty easy to argue that even the smartest among us has far more ignorance than knowledge. Even collectively, as a species with nearly 8,000,000,000 people currently living (and around another 100,000,000,000 who've passed before us), humankind is far from all-knowledgeable.

I know there were several times earlier in my life when I thought I had it all figured out. Invariably, the fall back to earth was a hard one. After four or five of these humbling events, I realized that it was time to stop the nonsense. I learned to listen more, be curious, ask questions, and speak less, but more thoughtfully.

So we need to accept that we have much to learn and be open to those who might teach us. You never know where your next great lesson is coming from. The Greek Stoic philosopher Epictetus said, 'We have two ears and one mouth so that we can listen twice as much as we speak.'

The point is that our perspective of reality will always be incomplete. And if everyone's perspective on reality is inherently incomplete, why not choose to foster a perspective that is a little more constructive? Such a fundamental change in how we think and how we see the world surely doesn't come easily or quickly, but it can be done.

Curiosity

One of the great by-products of accepting ignorance is that it spawns curiosity, which may be the most helpful trait in maintaining contentment. Curiosity keeps us in the moment and out of our heads. It helps us to keep things in perspective and learn. It helps us to stay humble and foster healthy relationships. This is covered in the previous section about the 13 Keys To Contentment.

Humility, Debate, and Compromise

Acknowledging our ignorance begets humility, which, in turn, fosters healthy debate and compromise. In our modern world of mass society, mass communication, and densely packed societies of polyculture, we need to navigate our differences and the healthiest way to do so is through debate and compromise. We need more humility to achieve this.

Not only is humility an appealing personal trait, but earnest humility sets the stage for personal growth and contentment. If you understand the holes in your knowledge and experience, you become more willing to learn, less ego-centric, more empathetic, and develop better connections with others.

These traits also apply to how you deal with yourself. The ability to judge ourselves with humility helps us settle our own personal issues and is a huge part of developing self-knowledge, gaining self-acceptance, and, ultimately, finding contentment.

Ignorance Of Others

With regard to personal contentment, the most important domain of ignorance we all must accept is that we don't know everything that goes on in others' heads. Sure, people express themselves in different ways, but we will never know the full truth about their intentions, experiences, and perspectives. This isn't to mention that not everyone is great at expressing themselves. Sometimes people choose words poorly, withhold thoughts, or are deceiving, intentionally or not. The bottom line is if you think you know what someone else thinks of you, you're probably wrong. More accurately, you're creating a belief based on your assumptions. On that note...

Belief

Sometimes we fill the void of ignorance with belief. As previously stated, it can absolutely get in the way of relationships when you believe that someone has certain thoughts that you don't know to be true.

Similarly, many times we also fill gaps of self-ignorance with a belief, too. It might be a positive belief that we have the capabilities to do things that we've never done before–things that make our goals and dreams achievable. But oftentimes our beliefs are negative–that we are incapable, unloveable, hopeless, and helpless, then these outcomes become more likely, as well. Although I would argue that a positive belief has less potential for inhibiting progress, both positive and negative beliefs are not grounded in the here and now. They are both a form of speculation.

If you become honest about your ignorance, you naturally become curious. If you become curious, you can question your beliefs and the underlying assumptions.

Whether it's a negative or a positive belief, believing it doesn't make it so. Questioning these beliefs about yourself is an important step towards freeing yourself to be yourself.

Dispelling a negative belief has obvious benefits. With no negative assumption to short-circuit our course of action, we are free to aspire, reach, and attain goals. We can change, connect with others, and have better days.

However, even a positive belief can restrict your potential. You might believe in some positive aspect of yourself so strongly, that you don't put forth as much effort to achieve a goal as you would otherwise. The result might be less desirable than if you dispelled the belief and simply gave your best effort. On the other hand, with hard work sometimes a positive belief can facilitate making your dreams come true, just as a negative belief can facilitate self-destruction.

Ultimately, if we accept our ignorance, we should have a clear humility not to assume things we don't know to be true.

Negative Assumptions

I'm not sure that making negative assumptions is part of a worldview, but it is at least a cognitive habit that can influence your worldview. Specifically, I'm talking about making assumptions that affect your self-image and your relationships.

When you assume the worst, days can be ruined by anxiety while you incessantly question something you said or did the day before, or the day before that, or even a week ago. Try as we might, we all occasionally misspeak or misphrase something. Ninety-nine percent of the time, it is harmless, and the other person never thought twice about it. Sometimes, situations are just difficult and the right words may not even exist to fit them. We tried, assumed we failed, then we spent days or weeks suffering through the replays.

Conversely, what happens when you assume the worst from an ambiguous text from someone at work or a distracted friend who didn't smile at you? You might think it's inconsequential, but no can act as though they haven't been slighted when they've assumed they have. Even if you manage to hide the feeling, the ramifications are that you likely won't interact with that person the same way as you would have if you hadn't made the negative assumption. It could simply inhibit you from doing the little things to cultivate the relationship like a friendly smile, a question about their day, or a birthday call. In this way, a negative assumption short-circuits any chance for a real connection with that person. It's a real shame when the odds are very likely the initial "slight" had absolutely nothing to do with you at all.

However, if we train ourselves not to assume the worst, give ourselves and others a little benefit of the doubt, and stay more in the moment, we won't suffer through the arduous second-guessing and destructiveness that comes with speculating on our negative assumptions.

Cognitive Habits and Underlying Assumptions

It's important to understand how negative thoughts work. When you react to a situation, you have an automatic thought. Automatic thoughts are simply the product of cognitive habits, including assumptions, and the beliefs they've produced over the years. If some of these thoughts lead to episodes of anxiety and depression, then you need to start questioning them.

Questioning Assumptions And The One Big Exception

As·sump·tion /ə´səm(p)SH(ə)n/ *noun 1. a thing that is accepted as true or as certain to happen, without proof.*

Questioning assumptions is essential to opening your mind, releasing possibilities, developing wisdom, and achieving personal autonomy. It requires curiosity, critical thinking, and humility. It is being open to learning. It is the opportunity to take real ownership and control of yourself and your well-being.

One of the predominant objectives in Cognitive Behavioral Therapy is to question negative assumptions, but we should question all assumptions. If the goal is to work toward the truth, then we should not take anything for granted.

The one exception I see for this is in giving a new relationship partner, either personal or business, the benefit of the doubt. This is very much making a positive assumption. I consider this to be an excellent way to foster connections and partnerships. Indeed, a small percentage of people will not honor your trust, and you will get burned, intentionally or not, but I think that the benefit of building a vast network of trusted partners far outweighs the costs of the occasional "betrayal". However, this also falls into the category of "trust, but verify". It is possible to give someone the benefit of the doubt while keeping an eye out for signs of bad faith or incompetence. Also, be sensible and don't wager something huge. It's one thing to do a small favor in good faith. It's another to trust your life savings to the advice of a new colleague.

Incidentally, there are times when we should also give ourselves the benefit of the doubt. This is especially true if you've gotten in the habit of making negative assumptions about yourself and your relationships. Have you really done anything at work that might cause you to lose your job? Did you really say the wrong thing when your spouse got upset? Your intent matters as much as your actions. Just because you may not have chosen the best words or had bad timing doesn't mean you should think the worst of yourself. Relationships are a two-way street. Give yourself a break.

Intuition

By definition, intuition is "the ability to understand something immediately, without the need for conscious reasoning." Some people call it "trusting your gut". It is important to know that there is no evidence that intuition is something magical or innately infallible. Intuition is an accumulation of your experience, which includes your perspective and cognitive habits, and the underlying assumptions you've collected over the years. Intuition can be wrong. It has areas where it serves you better–detecting danger or deception, for example–but it is not perfect.

I would never advise against never trusting your gut, but I would never advise against always trusting it, either. At best, it's one factor in making a decision that should also include other relevant facts you have at your disposal.

If you have a chronic issue with anxiety and depression, then you may consider giving your intuition a lot of critical thought. The many years of negative cognitive habits and assumptions have almost certainly infiltrated your core beliefs and skewed your intuitive thoughts in a way that is not only less realistic but more detrimental to your well-being, emergency situations notwithstanding.

<u>How To Question Assumptions And Keep Worries In Perspective</u>

Questioning assumptions and keeping things in perspective are cognitive habits. If you don't already practice these habits, then you have to develop them.

As I recommend so often, writing is the most effective tool in cultivating understanding and change in your personal development. At the end of each day, spend a few moments examining your thoughts on the day, noting the negative feelings you had and rooting out any assumptions made that contributed to those feelings. Write these down. Then, in the morning, review those assumptions and write down ways to question them. As your new day goes along, stay present and be aware of when your anxiety starts, consider the underlying assumptions behind those feelings, and make a note. Then jot down a few ways to question them to review at the end of the day.

Example—A phone call with your father resulted in anxiety because you think he didn't show enough interest in you and your life. Your assumptions were, 1) "He doesn't care about me", 2) "He doesn't think I'm good enough", and 3) "There's nothing I can do about it". Here's a way you can break it down.

At the <u>end of the day</u>, write your assumptions and include your supporting reasons.

<u>Assumption #1</u>–He doesn't care about me because I always have to call him and he never asks much about how I am or what I'm doing.

<u>Assumption #2</u>–He doesn't think I'm good enough because he never praises my accomplishments or tells me how proud he is of me.

<u>Assumption #3</u>–There's nothing I can do about it because he has always made me feel this way and he never changes no matter what I say or do.

The <u>next morning</u>, find ways to question the assumptions before you start your day–

<u>Assumption #1</u>–He doesn't care about me because I always have to call him and he never asks much about how I am or what I'm doing.

<u>Questioning this assumption</u>--Isn't it possible he does care, but not in a way that makes me feel like he does? Isn't it possible that is just the way his parents raised him, so this is what care looks like to him? If he has issues showing love or being self-absorbed, how is that my fault?

<u>Assumption #2</u>–He doesn't think I'm good enough because he never praises my accomplishments or tells me how proud he is of me.

<u>Questioning this assumption</u>--Did he actually say I wasn't good enough? Do I think this simply because I don't believe I'm good enough and expect that others see me the same way?

Even if he actually doesn't think I'm good enough, is it my responsibility to please him?

Assumption #3–There's nothing I can do about it because he has always made me feel this way and he never changes. Even if he doesn't change, can't I find other ways to feel better about myself?

Questioning this assumption--Rather than fight it, can't I just accept that he is who he is and not waste my energy on it? Why do I need him for validation? Can't I get validation elsewhere?

Questioning an assumption cracks the door open to the possibility that there is more to the situation than you first thought. Once you stop assuming, there are a plethora of other possibilities to consider, including those that are potentially closer to reality as well as those that offer greater control over your own well-being.

When these greater possibilities become part of your worldview, it also serves to give you a broader perspective. As you learn to question assumptions, be more curious, and be open to change, you will eventually learn to automatically have other questions that can help you. Things like, "Aren't there others who have suffered through things like this or worse who figured out ways to overcome it? What can I learn from them?", or, "How much has my upbringing affected my view of myself and what can I do to change my self-image? I didn't raise myself, after all."

Changing To A Healthier Worldview

I haven't seen a lot written on how to change your worldview. In my experience, the best approach is to make some changes in your life and start writing. The idea is to better facilitate a change in your thought habits by simultaneously making changes in your lifestyle, your environment, or your routine; anything to help put you in a transitional mode. It could be something simple like rearranging the furniture or redecorating, or something more dramatic like changing your job or relocating. Moving should be considered if you are surrounded by people whose presence in your life is making progress difficult. You could take up an exercise routine, a new hobby, or join a club. The idea is if you have external changes occurring in your life, your mind itself should be more accommodating to change. However, the heavy lifting is in the writing.

It could be a journal, poetry, blog, or song–but whatever you write, it needs to reflect positive observations on yourself, others, and the world around you. There's a short list below of small exercises that, if done daily, should help cultivate a healthier mindset more conducive to gaining control over your contentment. Be patient and persistent. This is an exercise in training your brain to think a different way. That doesn't happen in a few days or even weeks. If you make it a daily routine eventually you will notice change starting to happen.

You don't have to limit yourself to these daily exercises. Any type of writing that pertains to observing things like gratitude, beauty, your achievements, or things you like about people in your life will further cement the type of cognitive changes and improved worldview needed to build contentment.

None of this is to say that contemplative thought on its own can't be effective, but I think a combination of these approaches would be more effective.

Daily Exercises To Change Cognitive Habits And Improve Your Worldview

- List 5 things you are grateful for today–big and small, and recall specifically why those things happened and why you are grateful. These could literally be anything like a driver who let you merge safely, a nice conversation you

had with someone, or a cool breeze on a sunny day.
- List 5 things you found beautiful today–anything–a person, a deed, a sound, a blade of grass–anything, and recall the reasons why you found them beautiful.
- List 3 personal accomplishments–from bigger things like new jobs or finishing a marathon, to smaller things like making a healthy eating decision or putting the dishes away.
- List 3 assumptions you made and question them.
- List 3 things that you noticed that you haven't thought about in a while or ever.

You can come up with your own exercises, too. This is just a list that can give you some direction.

How To Change A Habit

It's not easy to break or create habits. We are creatures of routine and unlearning or learning habits takes time and persistence. Here's a little step-by-step that helps me.

1. In the morning, write down the habit you want to change and why. If applicable, itemize the part of your routine that you'd like to change. For example, if I'm trying to eat healthier, I would write, "Eat healthier–eat real food, not processed; eat only when I'm hungry; drink water between meals instead of snacking. Eating healthier will make me feel better, live longer, and as I get older it will be easier on my joints, I'll have better balance and can be more active". If I want to be more present, I might write down, "Be more present–focus on my immediate responsibilities and environment; meditate for 10 minutes at lunch. Being present will relieve me of anxieties and regret while staying focused on my quality of work and life." The act of writing this down every morning will help me remember better throughout the day.

2. Be present–if you're not in the moment recognizing when your actions need changing, it makes change harder because you're behaving unconsciously, not consciously. Focus on the here and now.

3. Be thoughtful–Take some time during the day to think about the motivations behind the habit you want to change. Understanding these underlying factors can not only make changing more feasible but give you new insights into why you want to change and how. I drive a lot and have a habit of eating in the car, so when I'm driving and thinking about eating, I think, "I'm just wanting to eat because I'm bored. I'm not even hungry. Drink some ice water instead."

4. Gain momentum one win at a time–Success begets success. Don't aim for the distant goal, win the moment. For instance, when you say "no" to junk food one time, the next time saying "no" will be easier. Win that moment and the next moment will be more winnable. The same applies if you have a habit of "beating yourself up" after you get home from work–for example, questioning an ambiguous comment from a co-worker and assuming they meant disrespect to you. If you succeed in stopping it today, then stopping it tomorrow is more likely.

5. Accept failures and successes–You're not going to win 100% of the battles, but be sure to give yourself credit when you do. Accept that failing is human and change is difficult. Keep trying.

6. Every day is a fresh start–It's important to realize that every day is a new day. Put the past behind you and start again with a fresh slate. "Every new beginning comes from some other beginning's end."--Seneca

Changing things within and without

When it comes to changing habits, we first have to actively work inward. I advocate writing. Whether journaling thoughts, poetry, songs or just reminding ourselves with daily notes, the act of writing enhances the power of our thoughts, which helps in changing habits.

There is no doubt, however, that we are also affected by our environment, and this includes the company we keep. Are the people we associate with influencing us in the right or wrong direction, or not at all? Depending on your personal needs, you may have to make some changes if you need to reduce friction on your path to change. This can be tough, especially when immediate family members might be a source of friction.

I'm not an advocate of "cutting people off", but rather taking the necessary breaks to give yourself the mental space you need. Everyone is human and I want to be available to help them, but I have to be practical, too. Whether this is for my own personal space, financial consideration, or because of a family dynamic, we have to take care of ourselves first before we can take care of others. Even then, there's only so much we can do for so many people. We can only do what we can do.

When working within, there are other techniques such as meditation and mantras. I think they can certainly help, but I think writing is the most powerful. Try a combination of them.

Changing things within ourselves can be hard, but changing the world around us, especially people, is even harder. Generally speaking, I don't recommend trying to change anyone individually. The situation is ripe with problems and people will just push back. But in a social context, there is ample evidence that sometimes our contentment is jeopardized more by accepting social norms than by fighting to change them. What if slaves and abolitionists hadn't fought to end slavery? What if unions and politicians hadn't fought for workers' rights and to end child labor? What if people hadn't fought deforestation and environmental degradation? There are good reasons and ways to change the world around us. This book doesn't address them, but I don't want to suggest that everyone should simply focus inward and accept everything else around them. We must accept the way things are, but we can still strive for change.

Small Steps

Goals and habits are more achievable when we focus instead on the small steps necessary to take right now. This is along the lines of the old Chinese proverb, "A journey of a thousand miles begins with a single step". What is the next thing we have to do? Figure that out, then do it. This is a part of how we live in the moment.

Taking action is important and a consideration we shouldn't take for granted. People get stuck for various reasons like perfectionism, paralysis by analysis, fear of failure, and uncertainty. Be mindful of where you are in the process of your plan. If you are stagnating, then take action, even if you aren't certain it's the right action. You can always adjust your course. Time spent doing the incorrect thing is almost certainly better than doing nothing at all.

As a writer, I know this mindset well. It is better to write something that you'll throw away than to not write at all. Get the gears turning and get something done. If it stinks or you fail, there are still lessons to be learned. At the very least, you'll know what not to do. The important thing is to take action.

Judgment

A lot of advice is given about "not judging". Although the intent is virtuous, I find this advice to be unrealistic. Of course, we judge. Judging is a survival tool. But just like pretty much anything else, if taken to an extreme, it can become destructive. Let's break it down a bit.

First, let's identify the kind of judgment we're talking

about. We're talking about judging people, not situations. Second, we're not talking about judging the rich and famous or strangers–that's gossip. We're talking about judging people who are in our lives. People whose relationships with us have effects on us. We're talking about family, friends, lovers, spouses, business associates, and neighbors. We must pass judgment because these people are directly involved in our lives. We care about them and our relationships with them. We use judgment to make decisions on how to proceed, usually regarding the well-being of the relationship, the other person, ourselves, or all of the above.

Three things come to mind in this realm of judgment.

1. Can you "walk a mile in another person's shoes"? Actually, no, you can't. Every person has a unique set of life experiences. How were they raised? What are their important life events? What is their mental condition? What are their genetic predispositions? You may share certain experiences with that person, but you will never completely understand the totality of influences that make up who they are and how they see the world. I think this is what people are likely talking about when they say "Don't judge". It also makes forgiving easier. It's better to "hate the sin, not the sinner", so lingering resentments don't accumulate and erode your contentment.
2. Judge people not on their mistakes, but on how they go about fixing them. We all make mistakes. We are human. Give people the chance to make it right before passing judgment.
3. Redemption is real. People can change. Old grudges don't just drag you down emotionally, they make you forget about redemption. Remember, redemption is something you might need one day, too.

The Cup Isn't Half-Full or Half-Empty

We've all heard the phrases, "The cup is half-full" or "the cup is half-empty". While this phrase absolutely indicates the influence our perspectives have on our state of mind, it also potentially steers us away from the direction of the truth.

Regarding the cup as half-full or half-empty is based on different sets of assumptions. If we make these assumptions regularly, the associated expectations develop. Once the expectations are set, we're getting into the world of speculation. I argue that too much of this, like judgment, can be destructive. Rather than see things as "half-full" or "half-empty", I think we should try to see things as they are, even if a particular truth may ultimately be unknowable.

Make The Best Of Things

"When life gives you lemons, make lemonade". This may sound like a "the glass is half full" perspective, but it's a little bit different. Taking lemons to make lemonade isn't simply a rosy view of reality, it is taking control to make the best of the situation. Crappy, unfair things happen in life. We have to accept that. We can still make the best of the situation, though, whether that's finding meaning from a tragedy, feeling gratitude for the time you had with a lost loved one, or taking a lesson from a mistake. Sometimes you have to make some lemonade.

Recreating Yourself

All the aforementioned aspects of changing and developing a healthier worldview are a big part of how we open the door to recreating ourselves. We can keep the parts we like, discard the parts we don't, and add new parts we desire. This is a process that takes time, patience and persistence. But we need a starting point we can use for reference not just to gauge our development, but to better inform our decisions on who we want to be and how to best recreate ourselves. We need our own self-image. So who are you?

"Be yourself. Everyone else is already taken."

-unknown

SELF-KNOWLEDGE AND ACCEPTANCE

<u>What is Self-Image?</u>

How do you see yourself? When you were younger, I bet you saw yourself "through the eyes of others". I'm pretty sure I did. Did you make your parents happy? Did you make your teachers happy? Did other kids like you? Did you have friends? How many friends did you have? These are the ways in which probably every child on earth forms a self-image. Are we accepted by our family and peers?

However, as we've come to learn, living solely to make others happy is a recipe for disappointment. Why? First, it puts your self-image entirely in someone else's control. Second, you are not responsible for other people's contentment–including, and especially, your parents, guardians, and mentors. You are responsible for your own contentment. They are responsible for theirs. Assuming the job of making others happy is a recipe doomed to fail. That doesn't mean you shouldn't be kind, thoughtful, funny, or understanding. Those are important tools in building and maintaining relationships. It does mean that if someone is trying to hold you responsible for their misery, you can't take it personally. They are simply wrong. Did you make a mistake? Everyone does at times. All you can do is apologize and do your best to make it right. If it's not enough for them, you can't let that hold you back.

Move on even if they can't.

A Balanced Self-Image

So what is a "balanced" self-image? It's one that's based on your judgments of yourself and also considers the expressed judgments of others. Do not speculate on other people's thoughts, only consider what they actually tell you. Even then, remember that what others say is not unquestionable. Others perspectives are flawed and incomplete, and their choice of words is subject to their motivations and limitations of expression.

Important observation–not only is everyone else's perspective of you forever incomplete and flawed, but your own perspective of yourself is also forever incomplete and flawed. So why bother at all? Because you need to start somewhere. Our journeys all need a starting point to gauge our progress and inform our decisions along the way. As we grow, we will learn more and change our view of ourselves and the world. That's how it's supposed to work.

Developing A Perspective On Yourself

When I was around 20 years old, I felt the instinctual urge to discover some things for myself. The culture I grew up in had instilled in me a set of beliefs and a perspective that I had never challenged. When you're a kid, you listen to the adults and conform to the way of life around you. It's not that my life was bad, it was that I didn't choose that way of life, and I was growing more and more aware of that. To feel more ownership of myself, I felt it was necessary to strip away everything and build my own philosophy of living.

Here's another time where writing really comes in handy, if not absolutely necessary. Whether you make a simple list of what you think your strengths, weaknesses, traits, likes, and dislikes are, keep a journal of your thoughts, write songs/poetry, or write a blog, writing will help expedite and maximize this process.

And I wasn't simply looking inward, I was also trying to understand the deeper meanings in life. At one point I remember thinking, "Well, a good starting point for the meaning of life must be good and evil. I'll begin there." It was probably months later when it occurred to me that maybe good and evil are the same thing, just different sides of the same coin. Like the same tool that could be used to create or destroy. I never came to a conclusion on this point, as I decided that trying to figure out unknowable things isn't practical.

I was drawn to writing poetry and songs and it was amazing how much I learned about myself during my early creative years. Not only did I get a better understanding of who I was, but I also could witness changes within myself over time. Reviewing what you wrote the month before will show you very clearly how your perspective and feelings have or haven't changed. Both results are informative and educational.

I also believe that any sort of written self-examination provides a kind of exposure therapy, getting us used to our own observations, both positive and negative, that may feel awkward at first. I think this is a very substantial part of this process. In a very real way, this is self-acceptance. You are facing truths about yourself and learning to accept them even if it's uncomfortable. It's kind of like hearing your recorded voice for the first time. Initially, it feels very awkward, but you get used to it over time, which is important to self-acceptance.

Even if you don't write stuff down, you can still develop a meaningful self-image. It would require being extra mindful of your actions and a keen memory of the portrait you are painting in your mind. However, I think that writing notes, even if only occasionally, really gives the whole process better traction.

Critical Thinking

Critical thinking is essential to a healthy self-image and living a content life. Not only does it help you make better decisions, it is a way of taking control. It helps you avoid others trying to influence you with lies, zeal, social and peer pressure, propaganda, or advertising.

Generally, critical thinking is defined as "objective analysis and evaluation of an issue in order to form a judgment." Obviously, no one can be completely objective, but I think that is the goal of critical thinking–to be as objective as possible.

This is my favorite description, "Critical thinking…is incorporated in a family of interwoven modes of thinking, among them: scientific thinking, mathematical thinking, historical thinking, anthropological thinking, economic thinking, moral thinking, and philosophical thinking." (From The Foundation For Critical Thinking's website.) I think this gets at the notion that you have to look at things from different angles in order to come up with a more accurate perspective on the issue at hand.

I think good critical thinking combines both accepting ignorance and being curious. It is seeing a hole in your knowledge and asking questions about it. And it takes practice.

Critical thinking is about fostering better judgment. And in the case of self-evaluation and evaluation of others, the better the judgment, the better off we'll be and the quicker we'll be better off.

Self-acceptance

Having a good relationship with yourself is not unlike having a good relationship with someone else. It requires things like patience, understanding, compromise, accommodation, effort, commitment, and acceptance. You are not going to be happy with everything you are and do, but to maintain the relationship, you have to accept yourself–for better and worse. For some, more effort will be required to accept your shortcomings. For others, it will be harder to accept your strengths. Both are important.

Self-acceptance can be aided by acknowledging the fact that none of us chose who we were born as. We didn't ask to be born with certain inherent traits and genetic conditions, nor did we choose to be born into a certain family or community. We have to accept that we were made a certain way and raised a certain way, and neither was of our volition.

Why is self-acceptance important? This may seem evident, but it's worth noting that to accept something is to consent to receive it. If you do not give yourself consent to be yourself, what kind of miserable existence is that? Not unlike being locked in a jail cell, I imagine. To consent to be yourself means you are free to be who you are and to become who you want to be.

Self-Actualization/Self-Being

Apart from self-knowledge and self-acceptance, I think the next step is self-actualization, although I don't really like the term. It seems to imply a stopping point or achievement. A better term might be "self-being". It combines "self-acceptance" with "being in the moment". I guess you might say it's like being a kid again, just with added knowledge and experience.

When I was going through this process, I was only following my intuition, not a suggested format. This is what it boiled down to–knowing who I was, accepting who I was, and then proceeding on my journey with added clarity and information as to what direction I wanted to go in because I knew myself better.

Flawed And Incomplete Self-Image

Just like our perspectives on the world are forever incomplete and flawed, so will be your self-image. That shouldn't stop you. You will still have much greater self-knowledge, giving you a great advantage in managing your well-being. Just as with any other endeavor, we will make mistakes. It is a learning process and our mistakes will teach us. Failure is a must. If we aren't failing, we probably aren't trying hard enough. Don't let missteps slow you down.

Another, more subtle aspect of a balanced, incomplete self-image is keeping our perspective on our place in the world. The world is a pretty big place with billions of people. It's so big it's hard for us to grasp And we don't really know about life in the rest of the universe. You are just one. This is not to diminish the importance of one person's role, but when troubles arise, I find it helpful to remember that I'm just one of billions on this planet and that everything is transitory and changing. It's probably best not to dive too deep into the existential end of the scale, but that is why we need balance. Yes, our lives are consequential and have importance, but let's not overstate that importance.

Self-Direction

Gone seem to be the days when parents let their kids make decisions and, therefore, mistakes. Many kids' activities and friendships are fully dictated by the parents, leaving the child as a bystander in their own life. It's little wonder that anxiety rates are on the rise as these children grow to be young adults with no experience in being self-directed, yet expected to navigate an adult world that can project indifference, animosity, and danger.

Part of the benefit of developing and accepting your own self-image is that you are taking the reins of your own life. Being self-directed is a very important step in gaining control. Once you feel ownership of yourself, your decisions, and your life, you begin to realize your power to deal with life's unpredictability and tribulations is much greater than you once thought. You also get to feel the weight of the consequences of your own decisions. This can seem unfortunate, but taking ownership of consequences, when justifiable, is far more educational, manageable, and constructive than not taking ownership of them. Failure really is the best teacher. As most will attest, there is no honor lost in learning the "hard way". It's going to happen, so accept it.

Failure

To belabor the last point a bit, failure is a part of life. It is a part of being human. Thomas Edison once said, "I have not failed 10,000 times—I've successfully found 10,000 ways that will not work." Reportedly, he had roughly 1000 failed attempts before creating the light bulb.

Few of us need this "inventor's mentality" in all its rigorous, tenacious, and deliberate scope, but we absolutely need to accept our failures and learn from them and not be ashamed.

Asking For Help

Given that we are a highly social species, why not ask for help? When I was younger, I let my pride get in the way and did not ask for help when I really needed it. My dad would offer to pay for a tutor to help me with a certain subject, and I would decline because I thought that getting extra help meant I wasn't smart enough. I later learned that not asking for help, well, isn't that smart. It takes two to teach–a teacher and a student. When the teacher has their own way of communicating a subject to a large roomful of students, odds are that there are more than a few in the room that aren't receiving the message optimally. It is no one's fault. We all have different perceptions. It's likely that the teacher's perspective on the subject is different than how some of the students will see it, once they understand it. But for them to understand it, they need a teacher with a similar perspective or communication style. So yes, now, when I need to, I ask for help.

No one is truly self-made. We all get a little help along the way. Like they say, it's not just what you know, but who you know. My dad used to call it "networking", which sounds really sterile and contrived. What he really meant was to get to know people. Make connections. People generally like to help each other. The more people you know, the more help you can get and give.

The Unexamined Life

"The unexamined life is not worth living."--Socrates

These immortal words from Socrates seem a bit harsh, but, after all, he was facing the death penalty for his philosophical convictions. Perhaps it was an "in your face" statement to his accusers, although that would seem out of character. In my opinion, he was stating that if we do not use the cerebral faculties that we possess, then we are not really human at all.

We have the capacity to uncover deeper truths and understandings about ourselves and our world. To not utilize this capacity to its greatest extent is a disservice to humanity, the world, and our own well-being. We must make the effort to learn and grow. We will all be better off for it.

Being A Friend To Yourself

"The defining features of friendship that are found in friendships to one's neighbors would seem to be derived from

features of friendship towards oneself."--Aristotle

I figured this one out before finding this quote. However, my observation is that your relationship with yourself is very much like your relationship with anyone else. Aristotle seems to think that your relationship with yourself informs your relationship with others, but I think the inverse can also be true.

Relationships require understanding, patience, commitment, trust, and a bit of transactional balance. I also believe relationships are best fostered when at least one party is willing to give the other the benefit of the doubt. Be the first to offer a little trust.

Humans are self-aware. We are able to think about our thoughts. This ability forms a type of dual-existence because there are times when we behave unconsciously–acting or reacting without thinking–and other times when we behave consciously. Because of this dynamic, we can form our own perspective of ourselves, thereby having a relationship with our unconscious selves.

Of course, because our perspectives are inherently incomplete, our relationship with ourselves will evolve, so it requires the same commitment, patience, understanding, and benefit of the doubt that any other healthy relationship requires.

In a way, when you are a friend to yourself, there are times when you can be your own counselor or therapist. This book has a lot of tools that might help in this regard, but just as a conventional friendship might suffer by being defined by constant "bitch-sessions" where the conversation always turns to life's daily dilemmas, failures, and disappointments, don't let your self-talk become defined similarly. You can have a balance where you take time to be serious and deal with life's unpleasantries, but don't take yourself too seriously too often.

Similarly, it is certainly possible to "have feelings about your feelings", where you can become stressed out about being stressed out, or sad about your sadness, for example. Stay in the moment and recognize this when it's happening so you can nip it in the bud.

Inner Dialogue (Monologue)/Self-Talk

I've read that as many as 70% of people have no internal dialogue. I find it hard to fathom that not everyone has internal discussions, but that's what the research shows. Apparently, many people communicate with themselves by images, not words. Also, many people don't engage in self-reflection at all, so no self-dialogue is happening.

I can see this as a problem. If you are unable to reflect on yourself, it seems you are limited in being able to discover the tendencies about yourself that are resulting in anxiety and depression, nor to discover ways to assess these and direct yourself towards a better life. Hopefully, though, many of these people are already content and have no reason to dig a little deeper to root out depression or anxiety.

PRACTICAL PHILOSOPHICAL CONCEPTS

Teachings From My Philosophical Influences And Teachers

I've read up on a lot of philosophies and religions and I've had a lot of teachers. I find a lot of useful pieces of wisdom from different people, but I am not a follower of a single school of thought. Whether it's my parents or Buddha, I only take the ideas that make the most sense to me and for me. I attribute this to my interest in practical solutions and desire for ownership of my perspective. This next section lays out some guiding words and philosophical concepts that have had the most effect on my life. It also contains some of my own thoughts.

Mom's Influence–Self-control, Acceptance, Self-subsistence

My mom was a very wise person and a natural Stoic. The best advice she ever gave me was, "You have to be able to take care of yourself first before you can take care of anyone else". The context of her words is important. In my younger days, I was a little overly altruistic. I didn't have enough respect for money, or myself. I would give both away a little too easily. Mom didn't want anyone taking advantage of me in a financial sense, but I came to realize that her words can be applied to all matters of self–mental well-being, physical well-being, and financial well-being.

Taking care of yourself doesn't have to be to the exclusion of taking care of others. At times we all need just to focus on ourselves, but a balanced approach where we are taking care of ourselves and others is likely the healthiest approach. Taking care of others not only fosters connections but can provide us with a valuable sense of productivity and purpose. As a young person, though, I needed to work on myself before I took on the responsibility of looking after someone else.

My mom's self-control was also very influential to me, although I sometimes wonder how much genetics play into that. I am her kid, after all. Regardless, she was a model of Stoicism and rationality and I think that her example showed me how to be content, in control, and present. She didn't let life's unpredictability and unfairness dramatically sway her. In large part because of this, she was a magnet for people. She was like a sun, and people naturally wanted to orbit around her. She radiated a glow of comfort and stability. She was also incredibly charming and welcoming. She made many people feel special by inquiring about them, taking interest in their stories, and making them feel good about who they are.

<u>Dad's Influence–Self-direction, Self-subsistence, Self-control, Acceptance, Friendship</u>

My dad is a very practical person and said specific things that I still use as guiding words today. While not as Stoic as my mom, he was always very present and taught me ways to be mindful of my actions.

He and my mom gave me a lot of room to make my own mistakes and didn't "pile on" when I made them. This isn't to say I didn't get punished from time to time, but, by and large, they let the consequences of my own decisions be the punishment. In doing this, I was able to learn how to live my life for myself, not for them, and learn to make decisions, live with my mistakes, and assess risk for myself. They fostered a lot of self-direction that helped prepare me for being an adult.

"Money isn't everything, but it sure is important". My dad likely told me this in response to an adolescent overture of liberal idealism. I've never been driven by materialism. I don't feel that purchasing things is going to make me a better or happier person. But I had to accept that some material things are necessary for modern living. I later paraphrased his comment to say, "Money can't buy you happiness, but it will buy you misery if that's all you can afford."

He taught me to conceptualize guilt and remorse as slightly different. "Guilt" is destructive, lingering too long and inhibiting forward progress. "Remorse" is feeling regret, but not debilitating. It's carrying the lesson you learned forward, not restrained by guilt.

My dad has also had lots of friends–all types. He has friends who differ from him religiously, politically, and in sexual orientation. He also has friends of different races, which may not seem noteworthy in this day and age, but in the early 1980s in the deep south, it made a big impression on me. One incident, in particular, made me very proud of him. My parents were both very social and often threw parties. At one particular party, in about 1980, my dad invited a black friend of his who owned a record shop and brought his wife. To almost everybody in attendance, this was no big deal. There were some older folks, however, who took notice and told my father they didn't appreciate him inviting a black couple. My father very matter-of-factly told them that if they weren't comfortable with it, they were "welcome to leave". My parents had already raised me to accept my fellow man, regardless of race, but this moment surely underscored the importance of it. Being in the deep south and doing what my dad did took moral conviction and human decency. I'll never forget it.

My dad also demonstrated to me a lot about acceptance of things–of people in particular. Even those folks at the party who he told were "welcome to leave". He didn't ask them to leave. In a very real way, what he said was, "I like you, but I disagree with you." In not asking them to leave, he was not just making a statement about himself, he was giving them the benefit of the doubt that they could make the right decision and not be racist. This was empowering to himself and, potentially, to his guests if they chose to wield that power to change for the better.

Jonathan Livingston Seagull–Individuality, Self-Direction, Curiosity, Failure

This book is one of my earliest philosophical influences. Like most teenagers, I didn't feel like I fit in. This book helped me value feeling different and encouraged curiosity. It helped me understand that it's ok to be me, to set goals, and to work hard to achieve them. Although I didn't realize it at the time, I think it also taught me the importance of humility, failure and not taking myself too seriously. We all fail. If you're not failing, you probably aren't trying hard enough. Fail, learn, then try again.

Buddhism–Mindfulness

I would argue that mindfulness, as many now call it, is something we're all born with, experience in childhood, and later is disrupted by our modern world as we become adults. Ultimately, many of us spend a lot of time, effort, and money trying to get it back.

Mindfulness is being in the moment. It's where life is lived. It's where contentment is found. In actuality, it is the whole of existence. Mindfulness is not worrying about what someone else may or may not be thinking. It is not focusing on past glories or regrets nor on the expectations of future success or failure.

It is necessary that we spend some time reflecting on the past and planning for the future. Learning from our experiences and thinking ahead are important survival tools. But true living happens in the moment. It's my home base and default mode.

Socrates–Accepting Ignorance, Pursuing Knowledge, Pursuing Self-Awareness

While I would argue the "Father of Western Philosophy" had some questionable ideas that were inherently informed by the era that he lived in, he was the first to plant the seeds of self-awareness and foster their growth by admitting ignorance and then pursuing knowledge.

"For I was conscious that I knew practically nothing..." Yes, it's worth saying again. When I first read this, it hit me like a ton of bricks. The most famous thinker in history admitting ignorance. I believe it is a key to personal self-acceptance and social wellness, not to mention that it is the truth. Without accepting our ignorance, there is no curiosity to pursue knowledge, no accommodation for compromise, no critical thought, no growth, and lots of stagnation.

I'll concede that there are probably some important figures in human history whose ego-driven ambitions led to achievements that were of some benefit to the world at large, despite their self-delusions that they knew more than they actually did. I know that for me, however, self-aggrandizing ambitions are not a path to contentment, nor does admitting ignorance undermine achieving goals in any way.

Curtis Mayfield–Equality, Acceptance

Curtis is one of my many, many musical heroes. Specifically, with regard to spirituality and philosophy, he had few peers. As one of the many respected voices of the Civil

Rights Movement, his messages resonated with me more than others. It wasn't just about change, placing blame, or resentment. It was about personal accountability, understanding, and the global community.

The recording of his 1971 performance, Live At The Bitter End, grabbed me and never let me go. From the joyous encouragement of We're A Winner and the admonishment of I Plan To Stay A Believer, to the Stoic call to personal empowerment of Check Out Your Mind, it is like a revival of human dignity.

My favorite song from that album is If There's A Hell Below, We're All Gonna Go. Curtis was a devout Christian, so I assume he presented this as a rhetorical device to tell us that none of us are perfect. We all have work to do. But I saw it a little differently. In my mind, the title was a message that none of us are better than the other. None of us chose to be who we are. We are all flawed. Live and let live. If you listen to the song, it is very specific to the era it was written, but this is how I interpreted the title.

Music–Mindfulness, Empathy, Self-Knowledge, Cultural Awareness, Self-Discipline, Change

Music is amazing. Listening to music can reduce stress, blood pressure, and pain. It can help you sleep better, keep you mentally alert, and elevate your mood. It can also help you through hard times and feel connected to others.

As a musician and songwriter, I've learned that playing and writing music is a great tool for fostering contentment in several ways.

Perhaps most importantly, musicians are "keepers of the moment". In order to have a good performance, you must be present even when you are playing a song for the 1000th time. Learning to play and perform well has an awful lot to do with being with the piece that you are performing, as well as being with your audience.

Another part of a good performance is connecting with the song's lyrics and music. Connecting with the lyrics, in particular, can produce feelings of empathy, which in turn can make the audience feel empathy. These connections are great for a sense of well-being.

In regards to songwriting, specifically as a form of self-expression, the act of spending time on your thoughts and feelings and writing them down is one of the best ways to learn about yourself. The years I've spent songwriting and discovering my own sound were key in gaining the self-acceptance I needed to be comfortable in my own skin.

Music is a reflection of culture, and being able to listen to music from people from very different backgrounds than myself opened my eyes to the diversity this world of humans has to offer. Even when the lyrics are in a foreign language, the music can reveal sensibilities that can help us understand each other better. The styles of music can also reveal musical knowledge that can teach me things and inform my own music.

And when it comes to learning an instrument, few things require the kind of self-discipline needed to learn to perform at a high level. Additionally, there are likely few pursuits where the 4 quadrants of learning are so clearly present....

- Unconscious incompetence–We are unaware of the knowledge and practice necessary to learn how to play well.
- Conscious incompetence–We've learned enough to know we aren't good.
- Conscious competence–We're not bad anymore, but we have to concentrate when we play.
- Unconscious competence–We can play well and don't have to think about it when we're playing

Unconscious competence is learning how to do something so well that it becomes your nature. Some people say this is "learning something so you can forget how to do it."

Stoicism--Control, Acceptance

Stoicism is an early Roman school of philosophy made famous mostly by the writings of Marcus Aurelius, Seneca, and Epictetus. Being "stoic" has a modern connotation of being emotionless, but that is not what it means. It means you have control over your actions and reactions to the emotional rollercoaster of life.

Stoic philosophy is a pragmatic approach to mental well-being. It is learning the difference between what you can and can't control, and exercising the control you do have. Importantly, you can't control the actions of others, but you can control your actions and reactions to whatever life hands you.

The famous "Serenity Prayer", attributed to theologian Reinhold Niebuhr in the 1930s, certainly has its roots in Stoicism as it sums up the cornerstone of Stoic thought.

> *God grant me the serenity to accept the things I*
> *cannot change,*
> *Courage to change the things I can,*
> *And wisdom to know the difference.*

This is how Epictetus phrased it in 108 A.D. "What, then, is to be done? To make the best of what is in our power, and take the rest as it naturally happens." He also said, "And to become educated [in Stoic philosophy] means just this, to learn what things are our own, and what are not."

There are many things we can't control like the weather, the actions of others, and the randomness of life, but we can control our actions, including our reactions to things in life we can't control.

The big gray area is society. We have to live together,

and in our modern democratic world, we have a say in how our society works. We can control our vote. Sometimes we want to influence the votes of others. Our desires for independence often clash with our natural requirements to be a part of the group and to serve social order. The best we can do here is debate, make our best arguments, give a little benefit of the doubt, and accept the results. Hopefully, we learn enough that in the next go-round our understanding is a little better, resulting in slightly different methods and goals, with better outcomes. We can achieve more if everyone would compromise a bit and not act as if their ideal image of reality is ideal for everyone else.

Personal relationships, including intimate ones, are another place where Stoic thought is essential. We must accept people as they are, but not at the expense of consideration of our own well-being. Over time, with regular negotiations, our love and support of another might result in some changes that make for a better relationship. Or perhaps the actions of another are too damaging and one needs to break it off to repair themselves. The relationship may permanently change, but we must be able to take care of ourselves first.

<u>Life Is A River–Control, Lack Of Control, Patience, Mindfulness</u>

Back in my 20s, my analogy was that life is like a river–at times casual and meandering indirectly, other times you have to paddle like hell to get through the rapids safely, or even worse, carry your boat around them. And rarely are points A and B connected by a straight line. You are in control, but not totally. I still like this analogy, but it doesn't hold the mystical weight of truth as it did when I was younger when I was reading up on Taoism, but I still like it.

The Gray Area

Absolutism–the acceptance of or belief in absolute principles in political, philosophical, ethical, or theological matters.

Many leaders, both political and religious, have wielded Absolutism throughout history, even to this day. Absolutism does not allow for debate. It does not allow for humility. It does not foster unity. It serves only dogma and political ambition. It is simply destructive, both to society and the individual.

Life is messy, complicated, and unpredictable. It isn't black and white. It is a million shades of gray. We need practical solutions to our modern problems that offer the most help to the most people. None of us have all the answers. We need to learn to open our minds, be curious, ask questions, communicate, and compromise.

Compromise–an agreement or a settlement of a dispute that is reached by each side making concessions.

A Bleeding-Heart Libertarian

As much as I espouse many Libertarian ideas such as autonomy, freedom and a general belief in "live and let live", I recognize that true libertarianism is an ideal, and therefore unattainable. Furthermore, we are an inherently social species, so notions of true autonomy, and freedom will forever collide with our social necessities.

Neil Peart, lyricist and drummer for the band Rush, who cut his philosophical teeth on the likes of Any Rand, was the first person I heard use the term, "bleeding-heart Libertarian", which he used later in his life to describe himself. I think it beautifully captures the messy nature of life and living, all those gray areas, and the tension that naturally exists between two human necessities–individualism and social need. I am a bleeding-heart Libertarian.

The Social Commitment

I'm sure this has been covered by others under a different name, but I'm calling it "The Social Commitment". The crux is that because humans are so dependent on their social groups that we, individually, benefit from the commitment and sacrifices we make to maintain the well-being of the social groups we belong to.

We are inherently a highly social species. Our individual well-being is inextricably tied to our society's well-being. In other words, if an individual suffers, so does society, and if society suffers, then so do individuals. In this context, "society" can be large, like a city, or small, like a marriage.

I would argue that everybody makes at least some personal commitments and sacrifices to their social groups in order to maintain and improve them. Part of this motivation is probably out of concern for other group members, and part is likely self-interest to maintain a social experience that benefits, or at least doesn't harm themselves. This seems to be how we evolved.

Now modern life has made us feel so much less dependent on others that our newfound affection for independence is often at odds with our still-existing membership in, and dependence on, social groups, and the commitments and sacrifices they require to be maintained. It is my hope that the pendulum will eventually swing back towards the center so that our social well-being will improve, thereby improving the quality of life for all.

No One Chooses Who They Start As, But We Can Change

Whether we are learning to accept others or ourselves,

this fundamental fact goes a long way in facilitating selfl-acceptance. It bears repeating. No one chooses who they were born and raised as. We cannot completely separate ourselves from our origins. It's not a bad idea to try. I tried to reset myself and learned a lot. However, one of the things I learned is that for better or worse, we were born with a body not of our choosing and into families and communities not of our choosing. Onward from there, the chain reaction of events is always tied to the beginning.

So when life deals someone a bad hand at the start, there is no ignoring it. When someone grows up seeing adults making bad decisions after bad decisions, there's a strong chance the child will grow up to repeat the behavior. It is not fair and does not completely absolve them of the responsibility to do better, but we can't escape the fact that none of us chose exactly how we were born and raised. This is something akin to separating the "sin" from the "sinner". Not only does this foster acceptance, but it makes forgiving easier, too, thereby preventing lingering resentments from piling up and undermining your well-being.

Balance

An unbalanced perspective might serve to provide the focus to reach a certain goal, like a single-mindedness that allows for no other consideration. I think of people whose careers require such dedication, time, and travel that other important facets of their lives, like family relationships, suffer. Perhaps their dedication serves the greater good, perhaps it serves vanity or both.

As far as daily living goes, having a balanced perspective allows for a more content life. Whether it's regarding how you see yourself vs. others, work vs. play, belief vs. truth, or relationships, I can't find any facet of living that doesn't benefit from a balanced perspective.

When I was younger and beginning to form my own perspective on my life, I became intrigued by the notion of balance. I could see balance in nature–how ecosystems strive for balance and how planets, solar systems, and galaxies balance on a point. Yinyang caught my eye and I started reading up on Taoism and the notion that harmony in nature is found in balance and that our best lives are to be balanced with and as nature. Striving for balance seemed evident in nature's way, and it had some inherent value to me.

This is not a new idea. Historically, this idea of balance is collectively known as The Golden Mean. It is the notion that the best path is the one between the two extremes. This idea is found in some form in most religions and philosophies. However, these days, in Western culture especially, we tend to think of polar opposites as being the only options–individual vs. society, nature vs. nurture, global vs. local, public vs. private, tradition vs. modernity, self-image vs. public image, or capitalism vs. socialism. The reporter asks, "So do you think it's this or that?" implying it must be one or the other when, in fact, it's likely some of both and other things, too. The point is that assuming only one absolute is correct represents a very unbalanced perspective and probably indicates a belief in an unattainable ideal. Reality is in between. That is The Golden Mean.

I think it's worth noting that achieving perfect, rigid balance, in itself, is an unattainable ideal. But just as with any other ideal, even though we never achieve it, we still must strive for it in the moment. The act of seeking balance is a constant way of daily life. It's the ever-mindful nudging of the pendulum towards the center when the forces of human culture and life are pulling it one way or another. It's something to be assessed from moment to moment.

What follows are many examples where I believe awareness and a pursuit of balance can be particularly helpful in living a content life.

Balance–The Middle Way

One of my favorite examples is in Buddhism, where the "Middle Way" is the balance between nurturing the spiritual self and the physical self. In a practical sense, this is balancing the need to nurture your spirit with the need to keep food on the table and a roof over your head. This really appeals to my sense of pragmatism. I don't relate to asceticism any better than materialism. I prefer the Middle Way.

Balance–Ideals As Guides, But Not As Goals

I believe that ideals are worth pursuing, but we must balance the need to strive for the ideal with the knowledge that ideals are unattainable. This is akin to "Do not let perfection be the enemy of progress". Just because life will never be perfect is not an excuse not to try. Much like the stars in the sky, we can use ideals for guidance, even though we know we won't get there. True success can only be found in the journey. The destination is an illusion.

Balance–The Truth/Approaching The Truth

As I've stated, no one knows everything, and this includes their real self. No one has complete self-knowledge. There is no such thing as a proprietary claim on the truth. Although ultimate truth is forever elusive, our journey toward it is real, even if our journey takes us in circles occasionally. The truth is out there. We will discover many truths on our journey, but not all of them.

Balance–Positive/Negative Worldview

Previously I suggested ways to adopt a healthier worldview. I think this is critical to daily contentment. However,

I would never suggest that a healthier worldview requires ignoring the ugly truths in the world. Bad things do happen, and ignoring it may offer some degree of contentment, but it comes at the expense of self-honesty and the connection with many human beings. We have to learn how to deal with negative events and then move on to achieve more positive things.

Balance–Belief And Truth

No one is or will ever be all-knowing. It is fine to have a belief, but it must be balanced with the knowledge that a belief does not mean truth. It may be true, but verifying it may be impossible, as in the case with belief in a god or afterlife. Or, sometimes a belief can be verified right or wrong given enough research. History is full of examples of beliefs proven wrong from the practice of bloodletting to the earth being the center of the universe.

Beliefs can twist your assumptions in a way that forces you to ignore the truth to satisfy your belief. For example, in the case of a charismatic political leader or a cult leader, if you assume that a leader is infallible, then you are forced to twist all your rationales to fit that. This is a disservice to the truth, reality and your autonomy.

Balance–Knowledge And Ignorance

Even the smartest people in the world are filled with ignorance. It's unfortunate that the word carries such negative connotations. It's a simple fact that we should all accept. Each of us individually, as well as the whole of society, would be better off if we each acknowledged and accepted our ignorance as well as our knowledge. Such an approach fosters humility and compromise. It is therefore fantastically healthy for relationships and society as a whole.

Accepting your ignorance also helps to keep your life,

including your problems, in perspective. However, those struggling with anxiety and depression may have an equally hard time accepting their knowledge. If you constantly question your self-worth, you probably discount the experience, knowledge, and wisdom you possess. It's important to have acceptance of both.

Balance–Self-Care And Care Of Others

My mom used to tell me, "You have to be able to take care of yourself before you can take care of others." Like the airline attendants tell you, "Place the mask on yourself first before helping the person next to you".

Does this mean you must consistently put your own interests ahead of others? No. I think it's tremendously important to get yourself financially and emotionally secure, but very few of us have the luxury of having that kind of security as a constant in our lives.

I imagine that there are very few who have the financial and emotional where-with-all to dedicate an enormous amount of time to caring for others. There are also a few who have virtually no resources to spare outside of self-care and support. But for the vast majority of us, it will be more of a balancing act, one that constantly requires adjusting this way and that as we try to make the best of our different life situations. There will be times when you must focus on yourself and times when you must focus on others.

I should also reiterate that taking care of others can provide a strong sense of purpose and productivity. But it can be taxing, as well. Work towards your balance.

Balance–Now, Past, Future

I firmly believe that living in the present moment, free of distracting forethoughts and afterthoughts, is where true contentment can be found. But we cannot discount the enormous value of thinking ahead and learning from the past. Still, we must balance these abilities and never stray too far and long from the present moment.

Balance–The Pursuit Of Pleasure

Yes, it is very possible to have too much of a good thing. Sure, we love to experience pleasure, but if we experience something pleasurable too often, we can take it for granted and it can lose its appeal. We become spoiled and unappreciative.

The poet Kahlil Gibran put it another way, "The deeper that sorrow carves into your being, the more joy you can contain." I take this to mean that sorrows are a part of life, and without them, the joy would seem less joyous. Again, without sometimes feeling pain and sorrow, the joy and pleasures of life would seem less meaningful.

Ultimately, a constant pursuit of pleasure is not a balanced approach and will fail to bring lasting contentment. We must accept and cope with pain and not try to escape it through pleasure-seeking, whether that's drugs, alcohol, sex, money, status, or anything else that is simply an external distraction.

Balance–Growing Up, But Not Growing Old

Growing up, or maturing, is a necessary part of life. I don't want to do it at the expense of losing all aspects of being a child, though. A child lives in the moment, is curious, and doesn't overthink things. These are the parts I loved about being a child. It's one of the reasons I still love being with children. I get a little vicarious feeling of being back there again.

I was fortunate to have a really wonderful childhood, so I know the good parts of being a kid. If you had a rough childhood, it may take some time to figure out how to wake up those good parts that you may have forgotten. But in focusing on being present and curious, I think we can all feel a little bit like a kid from time to time, even as adult responsibilities crash down on us occasionally.

Balance–Being Self-Aware and Being Self-Unaware

Being self-aware is the ability to think about your thoughts. Whether or not this is a uniquely human trait, it is a tool that humankind has elevated to a high level and may be the most important reason for mankind's world dominance as a species.

Being self-aware is largely what this book is about. The time we spend being self-aware is where we learn things, as well as unlearn some things, like cultural constructs we wish to discard and cognitive habits that are destructive or no longer useful. However, constantly being self-aware can potentially lead to neurosis. It is important to have time to be self-unaware; to simply be, experience life, and get out of your head.

As we learn these lessons and put them into practice, they become more and more incorporated into our being and become second-nature. During moments when we are self-unaware, these new habits function naturally, allowing us to enjoy our lives even more.

Just to be clear, being mindfully present is not relative to this topic. You can be just as present when you are being self-aware as when you are being self-unaware.

Balance--Patience

As laid out by Aristotle, patience is a virtue, but not if you have too much or too little of it. Too much patience can lead to stagnation, indecision, and resignation. Too little can lead to impulsivity, frustration, and anger. Both serve to add stress and undermine relationships with yourself and others.

Balance–Transactional Aspects Of Relationships

Whether we're talking about close friends, acquaintances, or business partners, there is always some transactional aspect to a relationship. Ideally, each side benefits from the relationship fairly equally which helps make the relationship a good one. These benefits can be emotional, such as really enjoying the other person's company or the other person taking an earnest interest in your life. Sometimes the benefits are actions, like favors or even gifts.

In addition to this transactional balance, I also think it's good to have a balanced perspective on why we do things for others. I believe in doing the right thing based on my own set of values. However, I don't want to be taken advantage of, either. My resources, including my time, are limited. If I sense the relationship is getting too unbalanced, I may temporarily disengage. I know in some instances it might be wiser to break things off permanently. I'm not a fan of this in almost any circumstance, but I can see why for some people in certain situations it is the best way.

Balance–Trust, But Verify–Others

This is an old adage and seems like a misnomer. Why verify if you trust? I think the answer is that you trust the source has good intentions, but need to verify because no one has perfect knowledge or motivations. I prefer giving a stranger the benefit of the doubt at least until they lose it. And, of course, an old friend is proven trustworthy. But both, like myself, are humans with ignorance, different perspectives and incomplete knowledge. Therefore, I need to balance my trust with a critical assessment to the information given by them to me.

We don't need to blindly accept everything we hear,

but we need to be open and incorporate the ideas of others to whatever degree our level of knowledge and wisdom dictates if we incorporate them at all. Advice on your car problem is less desirable from the mail carrier than from a trusted mechanic. However, the mail carrier could be right and the mechanic could be wrong. That's certainly possible, but less likely. Or they could both be wrong. We need to be aware of these probabilities and possibilities.

Balance–Trust, But Verify–The News

Although "the news" is certainly in the realm of the previous section, I think it deserves a separate mention given the modern age of communication we live in. "News" is all around us 24/7. It's on the TV, phones, computers, and social media. I think most "news" outlets strive for factualism, but due to time constraints can't present all facts relevant to a particular story. And there are some "news" outlets that clearly and intentionally omit some facts to adhere to a bias. We need to be aware of these dynamics when we're consuming the news.

Incidentally, I put the word "news" in quotes because most big media outlets engage in far too much commentary to be called simply the news. I believe this is primarily due to the desire to create sensationalism to increase ratings, thereby increasing ad revenue. Not-for-profit, information-based news doesn't seem to drive ratings, but we'd all be better off if it did. Or rather, if more of us watched it, we'd be better off.

Balance–Trust, But Verify–Your Intuition

People's intuition is not infallible. There is no evidence it's a magical source of divine guidance. Research suggests intuition is simply the sum of your cumulative life experiences crystallized in a moment. So, the older you are, the more life experience you've had, and therefore your intuition is probably better than a younger person's. Or if you have a ton of experience in a certain field, your intuition related to that field is probably better. Otherwise, don't automatically rely on "trusting your gut".

People who have a history of anxiety and/or depression need to be careful when listening to their intuition. Cognitive habits of negative assumptions, low self-esteem, and general distrust can negatively distort your perspective and affect your instinctive reactions to the world around you.

Our intuition is at its best when it's keeping us out of dangerous situations, research suggests. Other than that, you should take it with a grain of salt, in my opinion. At the very least, balance it with whatever relevant facts you have at your disposal.

Balance–Addressing Causes And Symptoms

I think this is a big cultural problem we have in the US and elsewhere. Perhaps it's because of our modern, quick-fix, microwave, instant-oatmeal society, but we've become far more interested in putting band-aids on symptoms and less interested in fixing what caused the symptoms in the first place. Fixing the cause of a problem is often more complex and time-consuming than just throwing a band-aid on it, but that isn't a good excuse for not trying. Otherwise, the problem never really goes away.

As author Anthony J. D'Angelo said, "When solving problems, dig at the roots instead of just hacking at the leaves."

Balance–What We Think And What Others Think

This is covered more in-depth in Section 4. We need to balance our adolescent inclination to care about what others think of us with a more mature appreciation of what we think of ourselves. As is indicated in the title of this book, it is perfectly natural for us to care what others think, but we need to give more equitable weight to our own opinion of ourselves in order to have a more well-defined self-image.

And this notion isn't confined to how it relates to self-image. It applies to anything we're debating or negotiating with anybody else. The truth is what we strive for, and no one person lays claim to it. But if we work together, we can get closer.

Balance–Self-Image And Cultural Identity

This was also covered previously, but needed to be included in this section, as well. Many of us carry a considerable portion of our cultural identity as a part of our personal identity. I don't think there is anything inherently wrong with this, but if it comes at the expense of inhibiting your personal growth, self-propriety, or relationships, then it can be a problem. And remember, you can't take ownership of your ancestors' or culture's achievements without taking ownership of its failures, as well. In fact, I argue that you can't do either because you aren't responsible for either.

I understand that we all feel the need to belong to a group, and that there are things inside each of us, culturally speaking, that are simply a part of us. We don't have to disassociate. But if we don't take the reins of our own lives instead of riding the coattails of those who came before us, we lose much of the opportunity to progress and find contentment within ourselves.

Balance–Whose Fault Is It?

I'm not a fan of the blame game. We all make mistakes. What's important is how we go about fixing those mistakes and avoid repeating them. Sometimes we need to fix mistakes made by others, which isn't fair, but life isn't fair and sometimes it's our best option.

With this in mind, I think it's helpful that when we make mistakes, big or small, that we understand that while we take ownership, the action was informed by our origins. This is a balanced perspective. This is not to say we are absolved of all responsibility, but I think it's unrealistic to accept majority responsibility for things we were exposed to in childhood, such as poor communication skills, low standard of family commitment, destructive relationship tactics, and especially trauma or abuse that have manifested in poor decisions you made later in life. The cycle is hard to break, but it can be broken. I would argue that breaking it comes easier when you don't shoulder all the blame for displaying the dysfunction you were taught as a kid. Better to start your day knowing that you can change. While it's unfair, it's up to you to do the hard work of steering away from the dysfunction and destructive habits you were taught as a child. That is where our responsibility lies. Let your regrets motivate you in this way, and not simply to beat yourself up.

Placing blame can also hurt your well-being by making you feel like a victim and undermining your control over your state of mind. If you are in the habit of blaming others, you're sending a message to yourself that your well-being is not in your control, it's in theirs.

Balance–Work and Play

I think we all have a different sense of what the balance is here. I think there is much personal contentment to be gained from both, but a main factor is likely how much you enjoy your work since we have to make at least some money. If you dislike your work, you probably feel the need to recreate more often. If you enjoy your work, then work itself is a type of recreation! Still, we all need some breaks to recharge our batteries and regain a little perspective on life. How you do it and how much is a personal choice and a balancing act.

Balance–Remorse

My dad gave me an important psychological tool when

I was a kid. While the words "guilt" and "remorse" are technically very similar, my dad conceptualized them differently, with "guilt" being the heavier of the two–the yoke of regret that you carry far too long, inhibiting your ability to move forward. "Remorse", on the other hand, is lighter. It is the reminder of a lesson you learned from a mistake, but not the mistake itself. So it is the lesson you carry with you, making your life better and helping you forward.

Another perspective on this construct has to do with balance. If we intend to truly learn from our mistake, then we never truly forget the mistake itself. It is a part of the fabric of our history. So the balance comes in remembering it, but not dwelling on it so much that we are unable to have good days and progress in our lives.

Balance–Relationship Interactions

Most relationships can't sustain constant discussions of weighty matters. There needs to be fun and laughter, too. Conversely, a relationship where personal matters of substance are never discussed will result in feeling more like acquaintances, not friends.

Similarly, most relationships probably need both parties to take an interest in each other. If one party is only interested in discussing their own lives but never hearing what the other has to say, then that doesn't make for much of a relationship.

Some relationships can become "toxic" for various reasons. Perhaps seeing that person less often is what you need at the moment. Perhaps you need to quit the relationship entirely for your own well-being. However, you should consider whatever unresolved issues may eat away at you later in life if you choose to disown someone, particularly if they are a family member or someone very important to you. Hopefully, occasional small doses are ok. Again, you have to find the balance.

Another aspect of balance in relationships is not losing your self-identity to your relationship. This means that you shouldn't become so wrapped up in your partner and the relationship that you lose your sense of self. I did this once and not only did important aspects of my self-identity become diluted and almost lost, but it soured the relationship. Be in love, but don't lose sight of yourself and the things that are important to you being you.

Balance–Perspective Between The Universe And You

I think one of the reasons that many people have anxiety and depression is that they have developed a chronic focus on their own issues that distorts their perspective of themselves in relation to the world and the universe. Your problems can seem enormous when you lack a bigger perspective. If you truly consider the enormity of the world and the universe, your problems quickly seem less important. We are very, very small.

This is not to say that each of us is completely unimportant. That's not true, either. We have to strike a balance between these extremes.

I think this is one of the reasons that psychedelic therapy for various mental disorders is becoming more and more common. When you take a psychedelic trip, it tends to give you a broader perspective of your place in the world and, indeed, the universe. It can take the pressure off when your personal issues become relatively smaller in your expanded perspective on reality.

Balance--Self-control And Indulgence

A good friend of my dad's, George Pollard, who lived to be a spirited 95- year-old, was fond of the Oscar Wilde quote, "Everything in moderation, including moderation". I guess it was his way of saying, "Live a little!". The balance point for this is surely different for different folks, but I appreciate indulgences more if I don't indulge constantly. And a life of constant moderation and self-control sounds exhausting and boring. This reminds me of another Pollard quote, "People ask me, 'How do you have so much energy at your age?' I say, 'I don't waste it all resisting temptation!'" I'm betting genetics had a hand in that, too!

Balance–Having Control And Being Emotional

Humans are emotional creatures. Some of us, more so, some of us, less so. It is certainly part of what makes us human.

However, we certainly aren't well served when our emotions run rough-shod over rationality.
Stoicism is covered earlier in this section, but it's certainly relevant here. Being stoic is not being devoid of emotion. It's being emotional, but being in control of your reaction to these emotions. A stoic tempers emotionality with rationality.

Balance–Virtues

In his book, Nicomachean Ethics, Aristotle put forth the idea that the primary key to living a good life was practicing morals. These morals are manifested in various virtues, such as patience, courage, generosity, etc. However, each potential virtue, if practiced in excess or dearth, becomes a vice. It is only when these feelings and actions are practiced in a balanced way that they become true virtues. I've paraphrased these to accommodate a more modern sensibility, but in a nutshell….

- Too much courage is reckless, too little is cowardly.
- Too much generosity is extravagant, too little is selfish.
- Too much patience is injudicious, too little is irascible.
- Too much friendliness is obsequious, too little is mean.
- Too much ambition is vain, too little is lazy.

- Too much modesty is shy, too little is shameless.
- Too much truthfulness or self-expression is boasting, too little is mock modesty.

There are others, but these were the most fundamental out of his list, in my opinion. To be clear, I haven't studied these enough to have an opinion on their overall importance relative to my concept of contentment, which this book is about. They seem to be engineered towards social constructs, which would understandably reflect the era. Still, they are an excellent example of how important balance is in how one lives their life.

Balance–The Golden Rule

"Do unto others as you would have them do unto you". Given the fact that we all have inherently different perspectives on the world, this is not a perfect rule, but I think it is still a good one to keep in mind unless you're a masochist. It's just important to remember that we are all different and that what is right for you may not be right for others.

DAILY LIFE
TOOLS AND
REMINDERS

Having a healthy perspective that facilitates contentment is practical life tool #1, but here are some other rules and tools that help me. I've reiterated a few that were previously mentioned.

1. Take care of yourself, then others–I think this is mostly directed at my young adult self. After I grew up a bit, I felt I had my personal self care more or less in hand. Since then, I've rarely felt my self-care was impaired by taking care of others. In fact, I felt a transition where I needed to take care of others to continue to learn and grow.

2. Feel and show gratitude–Simple "thank you's" go a long way in adding meaning to and fostering all your relationships, whether personal or business. In a larger sense, taking a moment or two every day to feel gratitude for a few of the things in life, big or small, that add to your well-being is an important part of good mental health maintenance. Importantly, note the reason for your gratitude. Do it until it becomes first nature.

3. You only can do what you can do–we all make mistakes, have regrets, underachieve, or over-commit. Accept the situation, learn from it, and move on. Similarly, we all

have limited resources. Contribute what you can and don't beat yourself up that you can't do more.

4. Be curious–Being curious helps us to stay in the moment, stay humble, learn, solve problems, avoid problems, foster healthy relationships, and accept ourselves and our place in the world.

5. Ask people questions–I love a good conversation, and it seems to be a dying art. I use one simple key–ask people questions. Learn about them. This goes for job interviews, too. Do your homework beforehand and make a list of questions that will give you a better sense of if the job is right for you. As a bonus, good questions will demonstrate your industry knowledge and professionalism, as well.

6. Separate personal criticism from job criticism–When I started in sales, I didn't know how to not take job failures or criticism personally, but I knew doing so would improve my job satisfaction, as well as my personal satisfaction and quality of work. Stay humble and learn to recognize when criticism is personal or not. Even when you think criticism is personal in nature, consider the source as to whether it's something to actually be hurt over. Otherwise, consider the criticism because it actually might be valid and something with which to leverage improvement.

7. Don't obsess over "What if?" scenarios–Obsessing over "what if's" is very much like assuming time travel is possible. #1–It's not, so stop wasting your time and energy replaying things over and over. #2–Even if time travel was possible, unintended consequences are a factor. Take time travel movies. While time travel movies are fun, we all have to suspend our disbelief twice to enjoy them. First, we have to believe that time travel is possible. Second, we have to believe that time paradoxes don't exist and that changing the past won't have unpredictable effects on the present. The truth is, we have no idea how changing the past would affect the present. Is there something you re-

gret? Fine. We all have regrets. Take the lesson forward with you and leave the regret in the past. You have no idea whether going back and fixing what you regret wouldn't make things worse now. #3–Replaying memories takes you out of the moment. Being able to reflect on the past is an incredibly useful tool for learning from history, but there is a point of diminishing returns and reflecting on the past too much can actually cause mental harm. Learn from the past and get back to the present.

8. Don't let perfection be the enemy of progress–Even if you don't feel you're on track to achieve your goal or the solution to the problem isn't ideal, don't stop trying. Even a little progress is important and you will learn lessons that will help you later in your journey. Similarly...

9. Don't let the fear of failure dominate–Fear of failure is often just your ego trying to protect itself from embarrassment. Sure, sometimes fear of failure can be really useful and actually save your job or your life, for instance, but often fear simply keeps you from learning and progressing. It is like being afraid to ask a question in a class or meeting because you're afraid of looking ignorant, or to start a new business or perform a new song you wrote. If you fail, you will learn. Nothing will grow your mind like failure. Learn to live with it and put your ego away.

10. Trust, but verify–As covered before, trust is vital to relationships, but beware of blind trust. Even if you trust someone's intent, that doesn't mean their advice or information is infallible.

11. Give the benefit of the doubt–This is such an important relationship-building tool. Yes, occasionally it will burn you, but you'd be surprised how rarely. Generally, people want to be trusted, and they appreciate the opportunity to prove themselves and build a relationship. Overall, I've found the positive results far outweigh the negative ones. Benefit of the doubt is warranted by the fact that none of

us has complete knowledge of the other's thoughts and feelings. In fact, we know very little. Some of us need to learn to give ourselves the benefit of the doubt, as well.

12. Apologize–When you make a mistake or hurt someone, intentionally or otherwise, own up to it. In fact, there may be times when you don't understand the perspective of the person you hurt, but because you love them and value the relationship, you should consider apologizing anyway. If you decide to apologize in this way, you need to follow up with some contemplative thought to try to understand that person's perspective. Otherwise, the apology isn't a true apology and nothing is learned, making it more likely for the incident to happen again.

13. Forgive–Just do it. Otherwise, the lingering resentment will just eat you up from the inside. To forgive doesn't mean that you absolve the person or group of the offending action. Forgiving means you're no longer angry. Forgiving is letting it go. Your relationship with the offending party may not last, or maybe it will. Either way, you're no longer saddled with anger and resentment. It helps me to consider the fact that nobody chose to be born as who they are and into the families that molded them in their formative years. Dysfunction breeds dysfunction.

14. Judge others not on the mistakes they make, but on how they try to fix their mistakes–I forget where I heard this, but I think it's one of the best pieces of advice ever. We all make mistakes. We're humans. Nothing and no one is perfect. It's how we go about trying to make things right that should influence our judgment of a person–including when that person is yourself. Incidentally, I don't see much use in passing judgment on someone unless I actually know them and I need judgment for my own or their well-being. Otherwise, judgment is just gossip.

15. Words matter–Be conscious about what you say and how you say it. If you think your words might have been mis-

construed, and it's important enough, double back with the person to clarify what you meant. Words are ineffective if we don't agree on their definitions, either, so consider this, as well.

16. Say "You're welcome", not "No problem"--My dad told me this once, and surprise, I listened! Yes, words matter, even if they are routine. When someone says "thank you", they are showing gratitude. Saying "no problem" dismisses that gratitude. Saying "you're welcome" accepts someone's gratitude. Some may not care, but if you pay attention to this, it will be appreciated by others. It will also help you to feel and show more gratitude, as well.

17. "Everything is going to be OK"--We live in an age when the basics of survival are all but covered for the vast majority of us. For most of the world, the days of famine and attacks by wild animals are no longer a concern as they were for most of humans' evolutionary development. If you or someone else is having a hard time, keep things in perspective and say, "Everything's going to be ok". Focus on the next step to move forward.

18. Wherever you go, there you are–As Bob Marley put it, "You're running and you're running and you're running away, but you can't run away from yourself". Yes, we are affected by our surroundings, but we have to be honest with ourselves when we see that the issue might be something within us. We must then proceed with the hard work of rooting it out.

19. Do It Now–When you're young, you feel like you have all the time in the world. You don't, especially after you have a family and other responsibilities. Take some of that extra time you have now and use it to pursue things that feel purposeful. You will likely have less of that time available when you get older with bigger commitments. Furthermore, don't put off difficult decisions or conversations. Give it the consideration it deserves, then rip the

band-aid off and get it over with. Otherwise, it can be a burden to you.

20. The importance of writing things down–This is covered more thoroughly in the first section of the book, but suffice to say that writing things down is extremely useful and helpful. From lists of everyday tasks to writing a memoir, the benefits are practically endless.

21. Fame and fortune are temporal and impermanent–I understand that many of us feel the need to be remembered after we're gone, but it is all fleeting. In my opinion, our best impact is how our life has affected others and positively influenced their lives and behaviors. This action has a ripple effect through society, and trickles down through generations. However long we're remembered is just incidental.

22. Money and material things can't buy you lasting happiness–Yes, purchasing things can provide some happiness, but studies show that experiences have far longer-lasting effects on your happiness. Pursuing wealth as a way to boost your self-image is a dead end. Yes, we need some money to survive, but to be seen as wealthy in the eyes of others discounts the importance of how we see ourselves, which has far more impact on personal contentment.

23. What you see on the TV and social media represents a tiny fraction of reality– Don't let your daily thoughts and decisions be overly influenced by what you see on electronic media. For-profit media is especially guilty of sensationalism and fear mongering because they know people feel compelled to tune in to that, ratings go up, and therefore ad revenue goes up. It does not represent a balanced picture or reality, much less the reality of your daily life. Marginalize it or cut it out altogether if you find your state of mind being negatively affected. Learn to be a critical consumer of the "news".

24. Turn off the TV and put down your phone–Yes, humans need to collect information and be entertained. On the

other hand, nothing distracts you from being present, deactivates your mind and destroys your productivity more than staring at your TV or phone. Remind yourself, "Does it control you, or do you control it?" Consider the shortness of life. Do you really want to spend so many of your precious, limited moments gazing off into a screen? Be present, aware of your actions, and make decisions in the moment that make your life better.

25. Move your body–Whether at work or play, a leisurely walk or a burning workout, physical health improves mental health, both in terms of brain chemistry and psychology. Stay active.

26. Communicate face-to-face or at least on the phone–As covered before, the value of non-verbal cues is often essential to delivering the intent of the message. That's why DM's, texts, and emails can be so misleading sometimes. You can indicate your positive intent with emojis and exclamation points, but there are certain conversations where you really must be face-to-face or at least on the phone. This is especially important for difficult conversations like break-ups, firing someone from a job, or sharing news of a death in the family. Even good news should be delivered more personally to convey the joyousness of a birth, a new job, or a relationship. We all need these moments.

27. Pick your battles–I've noticed this most in raising kids and being married. Your ego has a tendency to sneak in there just to validate itself that you were not wrong about the fact that, yes, you actually did tell your spouse about the kid's sleepover happening this weekend. Conversely, your spouse was not wrong about the fact you didn't. This is the dumbest shit ever. Who cares who has the better memory of what was said? This kind of incident is simply a battle of wills and egos, which will only serve to undermine your relationship. Don't sweat the small stuff. Let it go.

28. Maintain your self-identity in a relationship–I made this

mistake once. I got so wrapped up in the relationship that I lost all interest in the things that made me who I was. Not only was this not good for me but it was a major part of why the relationship failed. Find a balance.

29. Alcohol–I come from a family of social drinkers. Some of the best life advice I ever got was from my dad. He told me two important rules about drinking alcohol. #1) Don't drink alone and, 2) don't drink to forget your problems. Stick to these rules, and I think it's almost certain that you will always control your drinking, not the other way around.

30. Do you control it, or does it control you? Alcohol, drugs, gambling, social media, TV, eating habits, sex, work, exercise and other activities can be used in addictive ways. Whether we're trying to self-medicate, distract ourselves from unresolved personal issues, or just enjoying something too much, it's good to ask yourself this question–"Do I control it, or does it control me?" If the answer is the latter, it's time to take action to figure out how to regain control.

31. Stress avoidance and relief–Life can be stressful. There's no avoiding it entirely, but we can help ourselves avoid stressful situations by making better decisions through self-knowledge and self-acceptance. If you become good at living in the moment, you can dramatically reduce the stress you feel in anticipation and in the aftermath of a stressful event. You can also help relieve stress by taking baths, going on walks, drives, or meditating, etc. I think some stress eating is fine, as long as you remember that exercising relieves stress, as well, so go on a walk, too!

32. Indulgence–Sort of like the last point. Indulgences are satisfying and can help relieve stress, but remember that the more rare the indulgence, the more satisfying it is. Conversely, a constant indulgence only serves to dull the experience and likely becomes a vehicle for self-deprecation and increased stress.

33. Nature might be the best counselor–I'm not sure there is

anything better for your well-being than a nature walk. Despite the technical advances and spiritual longings of the human race, we came from nature and Earth is our home. Go out and explore it. Turn off your phone, go for a walk in the woods, and practice being in the moment. Turn your focus to what you see. Be curious. When any thoughts take you out of the moment, train your focus back to where you are, what you're doing, and what you see and hear. It also gives you a broader perspective.

34. Learn to entertain yourself–I had the good fortune to spend a few of my most formative years living in the country with virtually no neighbors. My memories are of jumping my bike over logs, playing with the dogs, throwing a baseball into a fence and exploring the woods. Inside, on rainy days, especially, I would play with my Hot Wheels or read Peanuts comic books. I don't remember ever feeling bored.

35. You can't make everyone happy–I grew up a people-pleaser, and I still am. But maturity has brought with it the understanding that if my efforts to please someone fail, I shouldn't take it personally. There is a comic strip I first saw when I was around 7 years old. A boy and a girl are leaning on the wall, talking.

Grumpy girl: "Why do you think we're put here on earth?"
Boy: "To make others happy"
Grumpy girl: "I don't think I'm making anyone very happy. Of course, nobody's making me very happy, either. Somebody's not doing their job!"

Of course, this goes directly to the heart of "owning your emotional state", but when I was a kid, I thought that making others happy was part of my purpose in life. It was something I was naturally inclined to do, whether it was to quench my insecurities or for the joy of it. Over time, though, I realized that tying my emotional equity to my ability to please someone wasn't just unrealistic, it was unhealthy. I learned to box it out. I still love making others happy, but I know that if I fail, it isn't something I should take personally and feel bad about. There are a thousand possible reasons that person is unhappy and my failed effort to put a smile on their face almost certainly isn't one of them.

ODDS AND ENDS

Is It Ever OK To Lose Control?

It is human to show emotion. Having stoic control does not mean being emotionless. Stoicism is tempering your emotional responses with rationality and controlling your reactions to emotions.

I would argue that it's never ok to lose control. I have lost control many, many times in my life. However, as I've broadened my perspective on myself and the world, staying in control has become progressively easier.

There are probably some benefits to "blowing off steam" occasionally, whether it be an angry tantrum, a date with a punching bag, or a bender. I wouldn't want it to harm others, of course. And I wouldn't want it to be the first option for dealing with a problem. We all have our human limits. I think the idea of developing more control is to stretch those limits and aspire to a place of greater enlightenment where blowing off steam is unnecessary.

Crying

Crying is an extremely healthy way to "blow off steam", and it's absolutely something you can, and often should, share with a loved one. We all need to do it sometimes, whether it's a few tears or a sob-fest. It helps us feel better and feel connected with others. And guys, ditch the toxic masculinity. Crying is constructive and restorative. Don't be afraid to cry when you feel the need to. It is good for you.

Grieving

We all deal with loss differently. The important thing is to deal with it, not avoid it. Some folks hit it head-on, others distract themselves. Some reach out to others, and some withdraw. Some people come to a standstill, others stick to their routines. Some are at points in between. Just give them, or yourself, some latitude. Tell them you care and support them however you can.

SUMMARY

Life is hard. Sometimes it can be very, very hard. There's no sense in making it harder than it is. When we rehash negative experiences from the past or have negative assumptions about the future, we are making life harder.

Life is for living. Be present. When you get lost in thought, mired in the past, or consumed with the future, you miss what is going on right in front of you. You lose curiosity and limit your opportunities to learn, grow, and build relationships.

Life is complicated. No one has all the answers. The sooner we all accept that, the sooner we can get to the good work of gaining knowledge, understanding, compromising, and progressing not only with others but with ourselves.

Life is always changing, often in ways we can't predict. We have to learn to cope with and accommodate these changes and all of life's uncertainties. Modern technology has changed our lives in countless ways and will continue to do so.

Life is unfair. For some, it is more unfair than for others. There is no healing in placing blame. Nothing is perfect, and we have to accept that and move forward changing what we can for the better.

Life is interesting. For every question answered, there are always more questions. Open your eyes and explore.

Life is beautiful. Beauty is in the eye of the beholder. Find what is beautiful to you.

Life is a journey. It is one moment. Don't miss it.

www.ingramcontent.com/pod-product-compliance
Lightning Source LLC
Chambersburg PA
CBHW070720130626

46553CB00005B/2081